Network Monitoring and Management Protocols: SNMP, NetFlow, sFlow and Telemetry

James Relington

DEDICATION

To those who seek knowledge, inspiration, and new perspectives—
may this book be a companion on your journey, a spark for curiosity,
and a reminder that every page turned is a step toward discovery.

AKNOWLEDGEMENTS

I would like to express my deepest gratitude to everyone who contributed to the creation of this book. To my colleagues and mentors, your insights and expertise have been invaluable. A special thank you to my family and friends for their unwavering support and encouragement throughout this journey.

Foundations of Network Monitoring

Network monitoring is a fundamental aspect of modern information technology infrastructures. As organizations increasingly rely on digital services and interconnected systems, the ability to observe, analyze, and maintain network performance has become essential. At its core, network monitoring involves the continuous observation of a network's components, including routers, switches, servers, and other devices, to ensure availability, optimal performance, and security. The origins of network monitoring trace back to the early days of computer networking, when administrators needed basic tools to verify that systems were online and functional. Over time, as networks grew more complex and business operations more dependent on them, monitoring evolved from a reactive troubleshooting tool into a proactive and strategic component of IT management.

Effective network monitoring provides visibility into what is happening across the entire network. It allows administrators to detect anomalies, identify bottlenecks, and respond to incidents in a timely manner. The real-time data collected from monitored devices helps to establish performance baselines and can be used to generate alerts when behavior deviates from the expected norm. This constant stream of information empowers organizations to maintain a high level of service quality, uphold service-level agreements, and avoid downtime that could lead to financial or reputational loss. In today's high-availability environments, where even brief outages can have major consequences, network monitoring acts as both a safeguard and an enabler of business continuity.

The concept of observability underpins much of what network monitoring seeks to achieve. Observability is the ability to infer the internal states of a system based on the data it generates. This includes metrics like bandwidth usage, packet loss, latency, and device availability. By capturing and analyzing this data, network administrators can make informed decisions about capacity planning, troubleshooting, and security posture. Observability also supports automation, as systems that are well-monitored can be integrated into broader orchestration platforms that respond to events without human intervention. For example, when a router begins dropping packets, an automated system might reroute traffic through an alternative path or alert engineers before users notice any degradation in service.

Network monitoring technologies are built upon a variety of protocols and methodologies that govern how data is collected and transmitted. In traditional environments, tools like the Simple Network Management Protocol (SNMP) have been widely used to poll devices for status information. As networks expanded and diversified, protocols like NetFlow, sFlow, and streaming telemetry were introduced to offer more granular and scalable approaches to data collection. These technologies differ in how they capture data, their impact on device performance, and the depth of information they provide. However, they all share the same goal: to provide actionable insights into the behavior of networks in real time.

One of the critical challenges in network monitoring is the balance between granularity and overhead. Collecting more detailed data can provide deeper insights but may also consume more bandwidth, processing power, and storage. Conversely, lighter-weight monitoring approaches may miss subtle but important signals. Administrators must carefully choose the right tools and configurations to align with their monitoring objectives. Additionally, with the growing prevalence of encrypted traffic and cloud-based services, monitoring solutions must adapt to maintain visibility without compromising security or violating privacy regulations. Techniques such as flow analysis, traffic sampling, and metadata inspection have been developed to address these evolving requirements.

The human element is also a significant component of network monitoring. While automation and artificial intelligence are increasingly being integrated into monitoring systems, skilled professionals are still needed to interpret results, configure thresholds, and respond to alerts. Understanding the context behind a spike in latency or a sudden drop in throughput requires experience and intuition that only human operators can provide. Moreover, as networks span multiple domains—including on-premises infrastructure, remote offices, and cloud environments—cross-functional collaboration becomes vital. Network engineers, security analysts, and application developers must work together to ensure end-to-end visibility and performance.

Network monitoring is not a one-size-fits-all discipline. Different organizations have different priorities, ranging from high availability in a data center to security visibility in a financial institution. As such, monitoring strategies must be tailored to the specific goals of the business. This involves selecting appropriate metrics, defining key performance indicators, and setting thresholds that trigger meaningful alerts. The design of dashboards and reports should also reflect the intended audience, whether it be IT operations teams, executive leadership, or external auditors. A well-designed monitoring system serves not just as a technical tool, but as a communication bridge that conveys the health and performance of the network in an accessible way.

The evolution of networks towards software-defined architectures, virtualization, and cloud-native deployments has further expanded the scope of monitoring. No longer limited to physical devices, modern monitoring must also track virtual machines, containers, microservices, and network functions virtualization (NFV). These environments are dynamic and ephemeral, often spinning up and down in seconds, which presents new challenges for visibility. In response, monitoring tools have evolved to incorporate APIs, agents, and telemetry streams that can keep pace with this rapid change. This shift has blurred the lines between network monitoring, application performance monitoring, and infrastructure monitoring, leading to more integrated observability platforms that provide a holistic view of the IT landscape.

Ultimately, the foundation of network monitoring lies in its ability to support stability, security, and scalability. By giving organizations the means to understand their networks in depth, monitoring enables proactive management and long-term planning. It helps to prevent issues before they arise, optimize resource allocation, and ensure that users enjoy a seamless experience. As digital transformation accelerates and networks become even more central to every aspect of modern life, the importance of network monitoring will only continue to grow. From the simplest local area network to the most complex global infrastructure, monitoring remains a cornerstone of operational excellence in the digital age.

The Evolution of Network Management Protocols

The development of network management protocols reflects the broader history of computer networking, marked by rapid innovation, growing complexity, and an ever-increasing need for visibility and control. From the earliest days of simple local networks to today's globally distributed, cloud-integrated infrastructures, the way networks are monitored and managed has undergone a remarkable transformation. At the heart of this evolution lies the continuous advancement of protocols that enable administrators to communicate with, understand, and control network devices across various environments. These protocols serve as the language between the management systems and the network infrastructure, translating technical performance into actionable intelligence and enabling the automation of many critical operational tasks.

In the earliest stages of networking, there was minimal formal structure for network management. Systems were relatively simple, and the primary goal was to ensure connectivity between a small number of devices. Monitoring was mostly manual, often relying on ping tests and log files to determine whether a system was operational.

As networks grew in size and complexity during the 1980s, it became clear that a more structured and automated approach to management was necessary. This led to the development of standardized protocols that could provide real-time status updates, performance data, and alert notifications across a wide range of devices and vendors.

One of the earliest and most influential network management protocols was the Simple Network Management Protocol, or SNMP. Introduced in 1988 as part of the Internet Engineering Task Force's efforts to standardize network communication, SNMP provided a relatively lightweight, vendor-neutral means of collecting and organizing information from networked devices. It operated on a client-server model, with a manager application querying agents installed on devices. These agents collected data from the devices' Management Information Bases (MIBs), which defined a structured format for various performance and configuration parameters. SNMP's early versions were limited in terms of security and functionality, but they provided the essential foundation for widespread, scalable network monitoring and management.

As networks expanded beyond isolated LANs and into enterprise-wide infrastructures, the limitations of SNMP began to surface. Version 1 lacked encryption and authentication, making it unsuitable for secure environments. Version 2 introduced improvements, such as bulk data transfers and better error handling, but it still fell short in terms of security. These shortcomings were addressed in SNMPv3, which added robust security features including message integrity, encryption, and authentication through the User-based Security Model. While SNMP remained widely adopted, particularly for basic device monitoring and alerting, it gradually became clear that polling-based models had inherent performance limitations, especially in large-scale or latency-sensitive environments.

To overcome some of these limitations, alternative protocols emerged to offer more flexible and high-performance monitoring capabilities. NetFlow, developed by Cisco in the mid-1990s, marked a significant shift in how network data was collected and analyzed. Rather than periodically polling devices for status updates, NetFlow enabled routers and switches to export detailed information about the traffic flowing through them. These flow records included data such as source and destination IP addresses, ports, protocols, and byte counts, giving administrators deep insights into network usage patterns and anomalies. NetFlow proved especially useful for capacity planning, traffic engineering, and security monitoring, and its basic structure influenced subsequent flow-based protocols.

As network demands continued to grow, particularly with the rise of high-speed backbone links and distributed architectures, scalability and sampling became more important. sFlow, developed by InMon, took a different approach from NetFlow by using statistical sampling of packets and counters. This allowed for monitoring of large-scale, high-throughput environments without overloading devices or networks with monitoring overhead. sFlow provided visibility across multiple layers of the network stack, supporting not only traffic analysis but also performance monitoring of CPUs, memory, and interfaces. Its vendor-neutral design and efficient use of resources made it a strong contender for large enterprise and service provider networks where performance and scalability were paramount.

As virtualization, cloud computing, and software-defined networking gained momentum, the requirements for network management protocols shifted once again. Traditional polling and flow export methods began to fall short in dynamic environments where virtual machines and containers could appear and disappear in seconds. The next stage in protocol evolution came in the form of streaming telemetry. Unlike SNMP or NetFlow, streaming telemetry was designed to push data from devices to collectors in near real-time, using modern transport protocols like gRPC and data encoding methods like Protocol Buffers. This allowed for more consistent, scalable, and low-latency data collection, opening the door for real-time analytics and more responsive network automation.

Streaming telemetry also introduced a stronger focus on model-driven data. With the use of YANG data models, telemetry allowed administrators to define exactly what information they wanted to collect and how it should be structured. This modular, schema-based approach improved interoperability and made it easier to integrate network data with external analytics platforms and machine learning systems. As network architectures grew more complex and programmable, telemetry protocols aligned more closely with the broader trend toward infrastructure-as-code and intent-based networking, where the state of the network is continuously validated against the desired outcomes defined by operators.

Throughout the evolution of network management protocols, one consistent trend has been the drive toward greater efficiency, granularity, and intelligence. Each generation of protocols sought to address the limitations of its predecessors while meeting the changing demands of the network environment. From the basic polling mechanisms of SNMP to the sophisticated, real-time data streams of telemetry, protocols have become more flexible, secure, and performance-oriented. They have enabled not just better visibility but also deeper integration with automation and orchestration systems, creating the possibility of self-healing, adaptive networks that respond to changes without human intervention.

The shift from reactive monitoring to proactive and predictive network management would not have been possible without these evolving protocols. As organizations continue to embrace digital transformation, remote work, cloud services, and edge computing, the role of network management protocols will remain critical. They form the invisible backbone of network observability, enabling administrators to maintain performance, ensure security, and support innovation across increasingly complex environments. The journey of these protocols is not merely technical—it reflects the broader evolution of networking itself, from static systems to dynamic, intelligent, and responsive ecosystems.

SNMP Architecture and Components

The Simple Network Management Protocol, widely known as SNMP, remains one of the most foundational and enduring protocols in the realm of network monitoring and management. Developed in the late 1980s as a response to the growing complexity of IP networks, SNMP was designed to offer a standardized and lightweight method for querying, monitoring, and managing networked devices such as routers, switches, firewalls, servers, and printers. Its architecture reflects a classic client-server model but is distinct in its terminology and operational flow. Understanding the architecture and components of SNMP is crucial to appreciating how it continues to support modern networks despite the emergence of newer and more advanced monitoring technologies.

At its core, SNMP operates within a distributed architecture composed of three primary elements: the SNMP manager, the SNMP agent, and the managed device. Each plays a specific and interdependent role in facilitating network visibility. The SNMP manager, sometimes referred to as the network management system (NMS), acts as the central control point. It initiates requests for information, interprets responses, and often provides a graphical or command-line interface through which administrators can interact with data. The manager is essentially the brain of the SNMP environment, tasked with collecting and analyzing the information necessary for network operations and troubleshooting.

On the other side of the communication is the SNMP agent. This is a software component running on each managed device that is capable of responding to requests from the manager and, in some cases, proactively sending notifications known as traps or informs. The agent provides an abstraction layer between the device's internal mechanisms and the SNMP manager. It accesses local system data through the device's operating system or dedicated interfaces and translates this into standardized formats that the SNMP manager can understand. This abstraction is what allows SNMP to function across a wide array of vendor devices and hardware platforms without requiring deep integration or custom development.

The third element in the architecture is the managed device itself. This is the actual network equipment or endpoint that hosts the SNMP agent and contains the operational data of interest. Managed devices include not only core infrastructure components like routers and switches but also peripheral devices such as IP cameras, environmental sensors, or industrial controllers. What unites all these devices under the SNMP model is the ability to expose performance and configuration data through the agent in a structured and accessible manner.

At the heart of SNMP's data model is the Management Information Base, or MIB. The MIB is essentially a virtual database containing definitions of the various data objects that can be accessed via SNMP. Each object is identified by an Object Identifier, or OID, which is a globally unique hierarchical value representing a specific piece of information. The MIB is structured as a tree, with broad categories branching into increasingly specific data points. For example, one branch may represent system information, while sub-branches may provide the hostname, uptime, or interface status. Because the MIB structure is standardized and extensible, SNMP can accommodate both universally supported data objects and vendor-specific extensions, allowing for both broad compatibility and customization.

Communication between the SNMP manager and agent is facilitated through a set of protocol data units, or PDUs. These PDUs define the types of messages exchanged in the SNMP protocol, including requests for data, instructions to set values, and notifications of events. The most common PDUs include GetRequest, GetNextRequest, SetRequest, and GetResponse, which together enable the manager to retrieve or modify data on the agent. Additionally, the Trap and Inform PDUs are used for asynchronous communication, allowing agents to alert managers of important changes or faults without being polled. While traps are sent without acknowledgment, informs include a response from the manager, ensuring that the notification was received.

SNMP supports multiple versions, with each version introducing enhancements to the protocol's architecture and security model. SNMPv1 laid the groundwork for basic operations and was widely adopted due to its simplicity. However, it lacked robust security features and supported only minimal error handling. SNMPv2 improved upon this by adding support for bulk data transfers and more detailed error codes, although its security model was still considered weak. SNMPv3 introduced the most significant architectural enhancements by incorporating a user-based security model, message integrity, and encryption. These improvements addressed long-standing concerns about the protocol's vulnerability to unauthorized access or data tampering, especially in environments handling sensitive or mission-critical information.

Despite its age, SNMP's modular and extensible architecture has allowed it to remain relevant. Its components can be deployed flexibly, and its simplicity makes it relatively easy to configure and maintain, particularly in smaller environments. In large-scale deployments, SNMP may be complemented by or integrated with other monitoring protocols, but it often continues to serve as a reliable source of foundational device-level data. SNMP's ability to run over UDP also contributes to its lightweight nature, minimizing the impact on bandwidth and device performance, though this also contributes to its statelessness and lack of delivery guarantees in earlier versions.

A particularly valuable aspect of the SNMP architecture is its support for hierarchical management. In large networks, it is possible to implement multiple layers of managers and sub-managers, each responsible for specific network segments. This distributed approach enhances scalability and reduces the burden on any single management point. SNMP agents can also be configured to filter or pre-process data before transmission, allowing organizations to fine-tune how much information is collected and when.

As network demands evolve, SNMP's architecture continues to face scrutiny, particularly with regard to its limitations in high-frequency data collection and lack of built-in support for modern encryption standards outside of SNMPv3. Nevertheless, the protocol's foundational architecture, with its clear delineation between managers, agents, and devices, as well as its reliance on structured data models through the MIB, provides a blueprint that has influenced the design of newer, more advanced telemetry systems. Its enduring presence in enterprise and service provider networks speaks to the robustness of its design and the practical utility of its components. Even in an era of cloud-native and software-defined infrastructures, SNMP remains a vital part of the network monitoring toolkit, offering a bridge between legacy systems and modern observability platforms.

Understanding SNMP Versions

The evolution of the Simple Network Management Protocol, or SNMP, has been marked by the introduction of different versions, each designed to address the shortcomings and limitations of its predecessor. Understanding the differences between SNMP versions is essential for network administrators and engineers who rely on this protocol for monitoring, management, and maintaining visibility into the health of networked devices. Each version of SNMP introduces new features, varying degrees of security, improved efficiency, and different operational mechanisms, all while maintaining backward compatibility to some extent. As network environments become increasingly diverse and security-conscious, the choice of which SNMP version to implement becomes not only a technical decision but also a strategic one.

The original version, SNMPv1, was released in 1988 and established the foundational structure and operation of the protocol. It introduced the manager-agent model, the use of Management Information Bases, and the basic set of operations including Get, GetNext, Set, and Trap. SNMPv1 was designed for simplicity and ease of implementation, which contributed to its rapid adoption. However, it offered very limited security, relying on a plaintext community string as a rudimentary form of authentication. These community strings, typically set as public for read-only access and private for read-write access, offered no encryption or verification of source identity. Despite these limitations, SNMPv1 was adequate for early network environments that were more isolated and less exposed to security threats.

As the internet expanded and enterprise networks grew more complex and interconnected, the limitations of SNMPv1 became more apparent. This led to the development of SNMPv2, which sought to address several areas of concern, including performance, functionality, and error handling. SNMPv2 introduced the GetBulk operation, which allowed managers to retrieve large sets of data in a single request. This greatly reduced the overhead associated with polling multiple variables, especially in environments with a large number of monitored interfaces or devices. SNMPv2 also improved error reporting with expanded error codes that offered more detailed information about issues encountered during communication between the manager and agent.

However, the security model introduced with SNMPv2, known as the SNMPv2 Security Protocols, was complex and difficult to implement. This version, sometimes referred to as SNMPv2p, never gained widespread adoption due to its lack of simplicity and compatibility. As a result, a revised version known as SNMPv2c emerged. SNMPv2c retained the enhanced performance features of SNMPv2 but reverted to the community string-based security model of SNMPv1. This compromise ensured broader compatibility and adoption, but at the cost of continuing the security vulnerabilities inherent in community string-based authentication. In practice, SNMPv2c became the de facto standard in many organizations, combining efficiency with manageable implementation effort, even though it did not adequately address the growing concerns around network security.

The need for a more secure version of SNMP that did not sacrifice usability led to the development and standardization of SNMPv3. This version represents the most robust and secure iteration of the protocol and is considered the current standard for secure network management. SNMPv3 introduced a comprehensive security framework built around the User-based Security Model (USM) and the View-based Access Control Model (VACM). These additions enabled authentication, privacy, and access control mechanisms that were entirely absent in earlier versions. Authentication in SNMPv3 is handled through user credentials with message integrity checks, while privacy is achieved through encryption, typically using protocols such as DES or AES. This ensures that SNMP messages are not only verified to come from trusted sources but are also protected from eavesdropping and tampering.

The USM component allows administrators to define user profiles, each with specific authentication and encryption requirements. For example, one user may be configured to authenticate with MD5 but not require privacy, while another may use SHA and also require AES encryption for all communications. This flexibility allows for granular control of access and security according to organizational policy. The VACM, on the other hand, determines which parts of the MIB a particular user can access. This allows for role-based access control, ensuring that different administrators or systems can only view or modify the data that is relevant to their function. Together, these two models make SNMPv3 highly adaptable and secure, suitable for modern enterprise networks where confidentiality, integrity, and controlled access are paramount.

Despite its advantages, SNMPv3 also introduces complexity in configuration and management. Unlike the simpler community string mechanism of earlier versions, SNMPv3 requires careful setup of users, security levels, and access views. This added complexity can be a barrier to adoption, particularly in smaller organizations or in environments where SNMP is used primarily for read-only monitoring. As a result, many networks continue to operate with SNMPv2c, accepting the trade-off between ease of use and the absence of strong security. Nonetheless, in sectors such as finance, healthcare, and government, where compliance with regulatory frameworks is essential, SNMPv3 is often mandated and considered a best practice.

In real-world scenarios, it is not uncommon to find all three versions of SNMP coexisting within a single network. Legacy devices may only support SNMPv1, while more recent devices may default to SNMPv2c or SNMPv3. Modern network management systems are typically capable of handling multiple versions simultaneously, using configuration files or discovery protocols to determine which version to use for each device. This hybrid approach allows organizations to gradually transition toward more secure and efficient SNMP implementations without the need for wholesale infrastructure replacement.

Understanding the evolution of SNMP versions provides valuable context for selecting the appropriate protocol for a given network environment. It reveals the constant tension between simplicity and security, between legacy support and modern best practices. Each version of SNMP builds on the lessons of the previous one, refining its capabilities to meet the changing demands of network visibility and control. Whether deployed in a data center, a remote branch office, or an industrial network, SNMP continues to serve as a critical tool for monitoring and managing the devices that form the backbone of digital communication. The choice of SNMP version directly impacts the security, scalability, and effectiveness of network operations, making it a fundamental consideration for any network architect or administrator.

SNMP MIBs and OIDs

Within the architecture of the Simple Network Management Protocol, Management Information Bases and Object Identifiers form the structural and semantic foundation that allows devices to expose their internal state to management systems. Without MIBs and OIDs, SNMP would lack the ability to describe, access, or organize the vast and diverse array of data points available in modern networked environments. These components are essential for translating raw operational data into meaningful, standardized metrics that can be monitored, analyzed, and acted upon by administrators and automated systems. Understanding how MIBs and OIDs function is central to effectively implementing and utilizing SNMP in any organization.

A Management Information Base, or MIB, is a collection of definitions that specify the properties of the managed objects within a device. These managed objects represent various aspects of the device's hardware and software state, including performance counters, configuration settings, and operational status indicators. Each managed object has a name, a unique identifier, a data type, and a description of how it behaves. The MIB functions like a blueprint or schema that tells SNMP agents and managers what can be queried or manipulated, how the data is formatted, and what each data point represents. MIBs are written using a formal language known as Structure of Management Information, or SMI, which is itself based on the Abstract Syntax Notation One (ASN.1) standard. This ensures that MIBs are machine-readable, platform-independent, and extensible.

The structure of a MIB is hierarchical and resembles a tree, with branches that descend from a common root. At the top level, the tree begins with broad categories such as ISO, identified by the number 1, and then branches into more specific domains such as org (3), dod (6), internet (1), and so forth. This branching continues all the way down to specific managed objects, each represented by a sequence of numbers known as an Object Identifier, or OID. The OID acts as a unique address or path to a specific piece of data within the MIB tree. For example, an OID like 1.3.6.1.2.1.1.5.0 points to the sysName object, which typically holds the name of the device. These numerical paths are essential because SNMP messages reference objects using their OIDs rather than their textual names, ensuring universal recognition across devices and platforms.

Each OID can represent a scalar object, which holds a single value, or a tabular object, which represents a table of values indexed by one or more keys. Scalars are simple and direct, useful for individual metrics like system uptime or available memory. Tabular objects are used for more complex data structures, such as the list of network interfaces or routing table entries. In this context, each row in the table has its own index, and each column is an object within the table. For example, the interface table includes entries like interface name, type, speed, and status for each interface, and these are accessed using a combination of the base OID and the interface index. This system allows SNMP to model multi-dimensional data in a structured and consistent way.

One of the most powerful aspects of MIBs and OIDs is their extensibility. While the base set of MIBs defined by the Internet Engineering Task Force, known as the standard MIBs, covers a wide range of common network functions, vendors can define their own proprietary MIB modules. These enterprise MIBs are rooted in the 1.3.6.1.4.1 branch of the OID tree, which is reserved for private enterprises. Each vendor is assigned a unique enterprise number under this branch and can then create custom MIBs that expose device-specific metrics and controls. For instance, a network switch vendor may define MIBs that include proprietary QoS metrics, environmental sensor readings, or chassis-level diagnostics. These vendor-specific MIBs can be imported into SNMP management systems to allow full access to advanced capabilities beyond the standard definitions.

MIBs are typically stored in text files with the .mib or .txt extension and must be compiled into a format that the SNMP manager can understand. Many management systems come with a predefined set of compiled MIBs and also offer tools to compile additional ones. The ability to import and understand new MIBs is essential when integrating new hardware into a network monitoring environment. Without the corresponding MIB, the SNMP manager may still be able to access OID data but will present it in an unreadable or unintelligible format, lacking context or meaning. When the MIB is present, the manager can display the friendly names, descriptions, and data types associated with each OID, making monitoring and troubleshooting far more effective.

Navigating and using MIBs effectively also requires an understanding of the semantics and structure of the OID naming system. Network administrators frequently encounter OIDs during the configuration of SNMP tools or while setting up performance thresholds, traps, and data polling intervals. While graphical interfaces often abstract this complexity, there are times when direct interaction with OIDs is necessary, especially when dealing with unfamiliar devices or troubleshooting unexpected behavior. Tools such as snmpwalk and snmpget are commonly used in these scenarios to manually query devices and discover which OIDs they support. By walking through a device's MIB tree, administrators can build a map of the data available and determine how best to monitor or configure the device.

Another critical function of MIBs is their role in SNMP traps and notifications. When an SNMP agent sends a trap to the manager, it includes OIDs that identify the event and any relevant variables. These OIDs tell the manager what kind of event occurred and provide context that allows for intelligent response, such as generating alerts, logging data, or triggering automated scripts. Without the proper MIB loaded, the manager might receive the trap but be unable to interpret it correctly, resulting in lost visibility or misdiagnosed problems. Therefore, maintaining an up-to-date repository of both standard and vendor-specific MIBs is a key aspect of successful SNMP deployment and operation.

SNMP MIBs and OIDs create the language that underpins all SNMP communications. They provide the structure, clarity, and precision necessary to manage increasingly complex and diverse network environments. By organizing data into a universally understood hierarchy and enabling both standardization and customization, MIBs and OIDs ensure that network devices can speak a common language while still offering the flexibility needed to support proprietary innovations. Their continued relevance across decades of technological advancement is a testament to the foresight embedded in the original SNMP design and a reminder that effective communication is the cornerstone of reliable network management.

SNMP Get, Set, and Trap Operations

At the heart of the Simple Network Management Protocol lies a set of core operations that facilitate communication between network management systems and the managed devices scattered throughout an infrastructure. These operations form the practical mechanics through which SNMP enables administrators to retrieve information, configure parameters, and receive event notifications from devices in real time. The fundamental operations in SNMP are the Get, Set, and Trap operations. Each plays a specific and vital role in maintaining visibility and control over a networked environment. Understanding how these operations work, their use cases, and their limitations provides a deeper appreciation for SNMP's enduring utility in the world of network monitoring and management.

The Get operation is perhaps the most fundamental and widely used function within SNMP. It allows a management system to retrieve the current value of a specific object from a managed device. This object is identified by an Object Identifier, or OID, which corresponds to a data point defined in the device's Management Information Base. For instance, if an administrator wants to check the status of a network interface or the amount of available memory on a router, they can use a Get request to query the relevant OID. The SNMP manager sends the Get request to the device's agent, which then looks up the OID in its MIB and returns the value in a GetResponse message. This operation provides the basis for routine polling, where monitoring systems periodically check the health and performance of devices to detect anomalies, track usage, and maintain historical records.

Closely related to the Get operation is the GetNext operation, which is particularly useful when navigating a MIB tree. While a standard Get request retrieves a specific object, the GetNext operation allows the manager to query the next object in the MIB hierarchy. This is especially useful when working with tabular data, such as a list of interfaces or routing entries, where the manager may not know all the OIDs in advance. By repeatedly issuing GetNext requests, a management system can walk through an entire table or subtree of the MIB, discovering all available data points in sequence. This technique, known as SNMP walking, is commonly used during network discovery and inventory processes, allowing systems to build a complete picture of a device's capabilities and configuration.

The Set operation, in contrast to Get and GetNext, allows the manager to change the value of an object on the managed device. This capability transforms SNMP from a passive monitoring protocol into an active management tool. For example, an administrator can use the Set operation to change the administrative status of an interface from up to down, modify SNMP configuration settings, or adjust thresholds for alarms. The Set operation requires both read-write access and appropriate permissions, making security and access control critically important. Unlike Get operations, which are generally safe to perform at any time, Set operations carry the risk of disrupting services if used improperly. As a result, they are typically used with caution and often restricted to specific trusted systems or user profiles, particularly when SNMPv3 is implemented with its granular access controls.

Security concerns have historically limited the widespread use of the Set operation in production environments. In SNMPv1 and SNMPv2c, the use of plaintext community strings for authentication made it possible for unauthorized users to alter device configurations if they had access to the network and knew the correct string. This risk prompted many organizations to disable Set operations entirely or limit them to isolated management networks. The advent of SNMPv3 introduced much-needed improvements by providing encrypted communications, authenticated users, and fine-grained control over which operations could be performed by which users. With these improvements, Set operations became safer and more practical in environments where secure and automated configuration changes are necessary.

The third key operation in SNMP is the Trap. Unlike Get and Set, which are initiated by the manager and follow a request-response model, Traps are unsolicited messages sent by agents to the manager when specific events occur. Traps serve as an alert mechanism, allowing devices to report problems or significant status changes without waiting for a polling cycle. For example, if a router interface goes down unexpectedly or if the temperature of a switch exceeds a critical threshold, the device can immediately generate and send a Trap to notify the management system. This asynchronous behavior is crucial for timely awareness and response to network issues, especially in large environments where constant polling of every parameter would be inefficient or impractical.

Each Trap message includes the OID corresponding to the event type and may include additional variable bindings that provide context or detail about the event. Traps are defined both in standard MIBs and in vendor-specific MIBs, allowing for flexibility and customization. Because Traps are sent over UDP and do not require acknowledgment, there is no guarantee they will be received. This limitation has led to the development of the Inform operation in SNMPv2 and SNMPv3, which functions similarly to a Trap but includes an acknowledgment from the manager, ensuring that critical notifications are not lost due to packet loss or network issues.

Despite their limitations, Traps are an essential part of any comprehensive SNMP implementation. They allow for immediate notification of faults and changes, helping to reduce mean time to resolution and ensuring that issues can be addressed before they escalate. Traps can be configured on devices to cover a wide array of events, including link status changes, authentication failures, configuration modifications, and environmental alerts. Properly managing and interpreting these Traps requires that the SNMP manager has access to the correct MIB files and is configured to listen on the appropriate ports, typically UDP port 162.

Taken together, the Get, Set, and Trap operations form a complete toolkit for interacting with managed devices in an SNMP-enabled network. They support both passive monitoring and active management, enable both synchronous queries and asynchronous alerts, and allow administrators to build systems that are both informative and responsive. While newer protocols such as streaming telemetry offer more modern and scalable alternatives, SNMP's core operations remain widely used due to their simplicity, reliability, and broad vendor support. A thorough understanding of these operations is essential for anyone responsible for managing networks, ensuring that they can extract value from existing infrastructure while laying the groundwork for future improvements.

Securing SNMP Communication

As networks have grown in size, complexity, and importance, the need to protect management protocols like SNMP has become critical. Originally developed in an era when networks were smaller and often isolated, SNMP was not designed with strong security features in mind. In its early versions, it relied on minimal and easily bypassed mechanisms for access control, making it vulnerable to unauthorized data retrieval, device manipulation, and eavesdropping. Over time, these weaknesses led to a growing recognition of the importance of securing SNMP communication, particularly as it became more widely used in enterprise and public-facing network environments. Addressing the security challenges inherent in SNMP has required a combination of protocol evolution, best practice implementation, and infrastructure design.

The earliest versions of SNMP, namely SNMPv1 and SNMPv2c, use community strings as their primary form of access control. These strings function as shared passwords between the manager and the agent, distinguishing between read-only and read-write access. However, community strings are sent in plaintext over the network, making them highly susceptible to interception through packet sniffing. An attacker who captures these strings can potentially retrieve sensitive configuration data or, in the case of write access, make changes to network devices. This poses a significant risk, especially in environments where SNMP messages traverse shared or untrusted segments of the network. Moreover, because there is no native mechanism in these versions to verify the identity of the sender or to ensure message integrity, they are also vulnerable to spoofing and tampering attacks.

Recognizing these risks, many organizations have historically restricted SNMP traffic using firewalls or access control lists, permitting it only between trusted management stations and known network devices. While this perimeter-based approach offers a basic level of protection, it is not sufficient in modern networks where threats can originate from inside the perimeter and where network boundaries are increasingly blurred by mobile devices, cloud services, and remote access. It also does not prevent attackers with access to the same local segment from capturing unencrypted SNMP traffic. These limitations make it clear that protocol-level security enhancements are necessary to truly secure SNMP communication.

The introduction of SNMPv3 marked a major step forward in addressing the security shortcomings of its predecessors. SNMPv3 incorporates a User-based Security Model (USM) that introduces robust mechanisms for authentication, encryption, and message integrity. These features help ensure that SNMP messages are sent by authorized entities, have not been altered in transit, and are not readable by unauthorized parties. SNMPv3 allows administrators to configure user profiles with specific security requirements, including authentication using HMAC-MD5 or HMAC-SHA algorithms, and encryption using DES or AES. These options provide flexibility in balancing security needs with performance considerations, as more robust encryption may require more processing power on constrained devices.

Authentication in SNMPv3 ensures that the identity of the message sender can be verified. This prevents spoofing attacks, where an attacker might attempt to impersonate a legitimate management station to gain access to sensitive information or issue malicious commands. Message integrity, also enabled through the authentication mechanisms, ensures that the contents of the SNMP message have not been altered during transmission. Encryption protects the confidentiality of the message payload, preventing unauthorized individuals from reading sensitive data such as system configurations, interface statistics, or trap notifications. Together, these mechanisms bring SNMP in line with modern expectations for secure communication protocols.

Implementing SNMPv3 requires careful planning and configuration. Each SNMP user must be created with a unique username, associated authentication and privacy settings, and specific access rights. Devices must be configured to recognize these users and enforce their permissions accordingly. This process can be more complex than simply assigning community strings, but it offers much greater control and visibility. Access control can be further refined through the View-based Access Control Model (VACM), which defines what portions of the MIB tree each user can access. This allows organizations to implement role-based access policies, ensuring that different teams or systems only see the data relevant to their function.

In environments where SNMPv3 cannot be fully implemented due to legacy equipment or software limitations, it is still possible to enhance the security of SNMPv1 or SNMPv2c by using external protections. One common method is to encapsulate SNMP traffic within a secure tunnel, such as an IPsec VPN or an SSH tunnel. This approach adds encryption and authentication at the network layer, protecting SNMP messages even if the protocol itself lacks native security. Additionally, using VLAN segmentation, private management networks, and strict firewall rules can help isolate SNMP traffic and reduce the risk of exposure to malicious actors.

Monitoring and logging SNMP traffic also plays an important role in securing its usage. By auditing SNMP requests, responses, and trap messages, administrators can detect suspicious patterns such as repeated unauthorized attempts to access devices, unexpected traps, or large volumes of SNMP Set operations. This data can be fed into a security information and event management system to correlate SNMP activity with other events across the network. Over time, this visibility enables organizations to fine-tune their SNMP configurations and respond more quickly to emerging threats.

The transition to secure SNMP communication must also include an organizational component. Security policies should clearly define who has access to SNMP credentials, which devices are managed through SNMP, and what operations are permitted. Regular audits of SNMP configurations, including the removal of default community strings, deactivation of unused SNMP versions, and review of SNMP user permissions, are essential to maintaining a secure posture. Training for network personnel is equally important, as misconfigurations are a common source of vulnerabilities. Administrators must understand the security implications of each SNMP version, how to properly configure SNMPv3, and how to detect and respond to potential misuse.

While newer protocols and technologies, such as streaming telemetry and RESTful APIs, offer alternatives to SNMP in certain use cases, SNMP remains deeply embedded in network management practices across industries. Its ubiquity and vendor support make it a necessary protocol to secure rather than abandon. Through the use of SNMPv3 and supporting best practices, it is possible to transform SNMP from a historically insecure protocol into a robust and trusted tool for managing the devices that form the backbone of digital infrastructure. As threats to network security continue to evolve, the importance of securing SNMP communication grows in parallel, requiring a proactive and informed approach that spans technology, policy, and operational discipline.

SNMPv3 User-Based Security Model

The User-Based Security Model, often abbreviated as USM, represents one of the most significant advancements introduced in SNMPv3. Developed to address the lack of robust security features in earlier versions of the Simple Network Management Protocol, USM enables a comprehensive framework for authentication, message integrity, and encryption. Unlike the earlier SNMP versions, which relied solely on plaintext community strings for access control, USM introduces a per-user security mechanism that gives administrators granular control over who can access SNMP resources and what operations they are permitted to perform. This model makes SNMPv3 a powerful and secure option for modern network environments where data confidentiality and integrity are essential.

In earlier versions like SNMPv1 and SNMPv2c, security was an afterthought. Community strings functioned more like weak passwords, offering little to no protection against eavesdropping, spoofing, or unauthorized access. With SNMPv3 and the introduction of USM, the protocol evolved into a much more secure tool suitable for enterprise-grade network management. USM achieves this by tying each SNMP operation to a defined user profile. Each user is configured with specific security parameters, including the choice of authentication method and whether or not encryption is enabled. These parameters are then used during communication to ensure that SNMP messages are coming from trusted sources and have not been tampered with in transit.

The USM operates on the principles of confidentiality, integrity, and authenticity. Confidentiality is achieved through encryption, which ensures that the contents of SNMP messages cannot be read by unauthorized individuals. Supported encryption algorithms typically include DES and AES, with AES offering stronger encryption and being more commonly recommended in current security guidelines. Integrity is enforced by hashing the message content with a secure algorithm, such as MD5 or SHA, and appending the result to the message. This hash is recalculated by the receiver and compared to the received value, confirming that the message has not been altered. Authenticity is verified by requiring the user to authenticate themselves using a password or passphrase that is not transmitted directly but used in conjunction with the hashing algorithm to prove the sender's identity.

The strength of USM lies in its flexibility and scalability. Multiple users can be defined on each SNMP-enabled device, each with different levels of security and access rights. For example, one user may be configured for read-only access with authentication but no encryption, while another user may have read-write access with both authentication and encryption enabled. This allows organizations to enforce role-based access control policies and to separate duties among different teams or systems. It also makes it easier to audit and manage access, as each SNMP operation can be traced back to a specific user account, unlike the shared community string model in SNMPv1 and SNMPv2c, where all operations appeared identical regardless of who initiated them.

To implement USM effectively, administrators must define a security name for each user and associate it with a corresponding authentication and privacy protocol. The user is also assigned a localized key, which is derived from the original passphrase using a hashing process that incorporates the SNMP engine ID of the device. This localization ensures that even if two devices have users with the same passphrase, the actual keys used for authentication and encryption are unique to each device. This prevents attackers from reusing captured authentication data across different systems, providing an additional layer of security. The use of engine IDs also helps prevent replay attacks, as each SNMP message includes time-based counters that are validated against the known state of the agent.

Another essential aspect of USM is its integration with the View-Based Access Control Model, or VACM, which further enhances the ability to control what data users can access and what operations they can perform. VACM allows administrators to define views of the MIB tree, associating these views with access policies for each user. This makes it possible to restrict certain users to a subset of the MIB, such as performance statistics, while denying access to sensitive configuration parameters. Combined with USM's authentication and encryption capabilities, this allows SNMPv3 to enforce a high degree of security and access control tailored to the needs of the organization.

One of the challenges of implementing USM is its relative complexity compared to the simplicity of community string-based models. Setting up SNMPv3 with USM requires detailed configuration on both the management station and the managed devices, including user creation, security level definition, and key synchronization. Tools and documentation must be carefully followed to ensure that keys are derived and stored correctly and that both ends of the communication path are using compatible parameters. Despite this complexity, the security benefits far outweigh the initial learning curve, especially in environments where data protection is a top priority.

Operationally, USM allows SNMPv3 to support three security levels: noAuthNoPriv, authNoPriv, and authPriv. These levels correspond to configurations that offer no authentication or encryption, authentication without encryption, and both authentication and encryption, respectively. By offering these tiers, SNMPv3 can be deployed with varying degrees of security depending on the sensitivity of the environment. For example, in a trusted internal network, a user might be granted access with only authentication, while in a high-security context such as a data center or financial institution, both authentication and encryption would be mandatory. This level of granularity ensures that SNMPv3 can be adapted to a wide variety of use cases while maintaining a secure baseline.

The use of USM also improves accountability within the network management process. Because each SNMP request is tied to a specific user, audit logs can reflect precisely who performed each action, what data was accessed, and when the operation occurred. This is particularly important in regulated industries where change tracking and forensic analysis are required for compliance. It also helps in troubleshooting and internal security investigations, as anomalous activity can be traced back to individual users rather than ambiguous shared credentials.

The User-Based Security Model has become an integral part of secure network operations. As threats to network infrastructure continue to evolve, the necessity of strong, user-specific controls at the protocol level becomes increasingly apparent. USM empowers administrators to define and enforce access policies with precision, ensures that sensitive network data is protected in transit, and supports the growing need for secure automation in complex environments. Its introduction represents a significant leap forward in the maturity of SNMP, aligning it with modern security expectations while preserving the protocol's core strengths of simplicity and interoperability. Through the adoption and correct implementation of USM, organizations can transform SNMP from a legacy protocol into a secure and reliable component of their network management strategy.

Practical SNMP Deployment Scenarios

Deploying SNMP in real-world network environments requires more than a basic understanding of the protocol. While the theoretical foundations are important, the true value of SNMP is revealed through practical deployment strategies that account for the scale, purpose, and security needs of specific environments. SNMP is widely supported by nearly every network-capable device, making it one of the most versatile and adaptable protocols in the administrator's toolkit. However, achieving effective monitoring and management depends on making informed decisions regarding SNMP version selection, MIB utilization, polling strategies, access control, and integration with other systems. Across a variety of network topologies, SNMP can be tailored to support both simple and complex operational needs.

In small office networks, SNMP is typically used to monitor the health of a handful of core devices such as switches, routers, printers, and access points. These environments often rely on SNMPv2c due to its simplicity and ease of setup. A single network management system may poll the devices at regular intervals to retrieve metrics like CPU usage, interface status, and available memory. SNMP traps might be enabled on critical devices to alert administrators of sudden changes, such as link failures or hardware malfunctions. The configuration is usually straightforward, with community strings defined for read-only access and basic firewall rules restricting SNMP traffic to authorized management hosts. Although this approach lacks the advanced security of SNMPv3, it is often sufficient for smaller networks where exposure is limited, and the threat landscape is relatively controlled.

In medium-sized enterprise environments, SNMP plays a more central role in maintaining visibility across multiple departments, buildings, or branch offices. The complexity of such networks demands a more organized approach to SNMP deployment. Devices are grouped into logical segments, and polling is scheduled to avoid overloading network links or device CPUs. Management systems are typically distributed, with a centralized platform aggregating and correlating data from different locations. Redundancy and failover are often built into the monitoring infrastructure to ensure continuous visibility even if one system fails. In this context, SNMPv3 becomes more viable due to its enhanced security features, especially when dealing with remote sites connected over public or semi-public networks. User-based access control ensures that different teams or service providers have access only to the data they need, reducing the risk of misconfiguration or data exposure.

Large enterprise and service provider networks present even greater challenges that require highly scalable and secure SNMP deployments. Thousands of devices must be monitored across data centers, campuses, and geographically dispersed branches. The volume of SNMP traffic alone can become significant, particularly when frequent polling is used. To manage this, administrators often implement distributed polling engines located close to the devices they monitor. These engines forward their collected data to a centralized collector or analysis platform. This architecture reduces latency, conserves bandwidth, and improves performance. Devices are typically configured to support SNMPv3, with encryption and authentication enabled. Role-based access is strictly enforced, and SNMP traps are configured to report only high-priority events to reduce noise and false alarms. Network segmentation is also used to isolate management traffic from production and user data, enhancing security and reliability.

In data centers, SNMP is critical for monitoring physical and virtual infrastructure alike. Environmental sensors report temperature, humidity, and power consumption, helping to maintain optimal operating conditions and prevent hardware damage. Switches and routers expose performance counters, interface errors, and routing table changes. Virtualization platforms often support SNMP through their hypervisor management interfaces, allowing for the monitoring of virtual machines, host performance, and storage usage. SNMP data is collected by sophisticated network management systems that integrate with other monitoring tools such as syslog servers, NetFlow collectors, and SIEM platforms. Correlation between SNMP traps and logs allows for detailed event reconstruction and faster root cause analysis. In these high-density environments, careful tuning of polling intervals and MIB selection is necessary to minimize overhead while maximizing insight.

Campus networks present a different set of SNMP deployment scenarios focused on user access, mobility, and edge device monitoring. Wireless controllers, access points, and edge switches are frequently monitored using SNMP to ensure consistent user experience and rapid response to service disruptions. Traps and polling are used in tandem to detect rogue devices, port flapping, or power issues in PoE deployments. SNMP is also employed in network access control solutions, where it integrates with RADIUS and DHCP systems to enforce policies and isolate unauthorized endpoints. SNMPv3 is typically used on core and distribution devices, while SNMPv2c may still be present on legacy or edge hardware due to compatibility constraints. Access control lists and VPN tunnels are implemented to secure SNMP traffic, especially when remote management is performed from central IT offices.

Another practical deployment scenario involves using SNMP in industrial environments, where it coexists with specialized protocols like Modbus, DNP3, or BACnet. Here, SNMP serves as a bridge between operational technology and IT, enabling centralized monitoring of critical infrastructure such as power systems, HVAC units, and manufacturing equipment. These deployments often rely on vendor-specific MIBs to expose detailed metrics that are not covered by standard SNMP definitions. The simplicity and low bandwidth requirements of SNMP make it well-suited for environments where resources are constrained, and reliability is essential. However, the need for security is heightened in these scenarios due to the potential impact of compromised devices on physical operations. SNMPv3 with encrypted communication is strongly recommended, and network segmentation is enforced to keep OT traffic separate from general enterprise traffic.

In cloud-based and hybrid environments, SNMP remains a relevant protocol even as newer APIs and telemetry solutions gain prominence. Virtual appliances, VPN concentrators, firewalls, and cloud-hosted routers still expose SNMP interfaces for legacy compatibility and integration with existing monitoring platforms. SNMP is often used in conjunction with cloud-native tools, enabling organizations to transition gradually while retaining visibility into their traditional infrastructure. Secure tunnels or cloud management gateways are used to collect SNMP data from cloud-hosted instances and transmit it securely to on-premises systems. These scenarios highlight the protocol's adaptability and continued importance in bridging the gap between old and new infrastructure paradigms.

Across all these deployment scenarios, SNMP proves to be a highly adaptable and valuable protocol for network monitoring and management. Its ability to operate across diverse devices, vendors, and platforms ensures that it remains a key component of any network administrator's strategy. By applying best practices, leveraging SNMPv3 for security, and integrating SNMP data with broader IT management systems, organizations can build robust monitoring solutions capable of supporting the demands of modern networking. Whether in small offices, global enterprises, or industrial control systems, SNMP provides the visibility and control necessary to ensure operational efficiency, reliability, and security.

Troubleshooting SNMP Environments

Maintaining a functional SNMP environment is essential for consistent visibility and effective network management, but even the most carefully deployed systems can encounter issues. Troubleshooting SNMP problems requires a solid understanding of the protocol's components, communication model, and the way different devices and management systems interact. While SNMP is a relatively lightweight and straightforward protocol, its reliance on proper configuration, secure communication, and consistent behavior across heterogeneous devices introduces many potential points of failure. Identifying and resolving these problems demands a methodical approach that balances protocol-level investigation with device-specific diagnostics and management system verification.

One of the most common issues encountered in SNMP environments is the inability of the management system to communicate with a device. This basic connectivity problem can stem from several causes, beginning with network layer issues. If the SNMP manager cannot reach the IP address of the device due to routing problems, firewall rules, or interface misconfigurations, no SNMP operation can be performed. Verifying connectivity with ping or traceroute tools is a first step, but this only confirms IP reachability. Beyond that, administrators need to ensure that the correct UDP port is open on the device and that it is listening for SNMP queries. SNMP typically uses UDP port 161 for polling and port 162 for receiving traps, and if these ports are blocked or filtered, communication will fail silently.

Assuming connectivity is intact, the next troubleshooting focus is often authentication and access control. In SNMPv1 and SNMPv2c environments, mismatched community strings are a frequent culprit. If the SNMP manager is configured with a community string that does not match the one expected by the device, queries will be ignored or rejected. This can lead to frustration, especially when no error message is returned and the management system simply displays empty results or times out. Carefully verifying that the community strings match exactly, including case sensitivity, is essential. In SNMPv3 environments, authentication becomes more complex, involving usernames, authentication protocols, privacy settings, and localized keys. A mismatch in any of these parameters can cause the communication to fail. Debugging SNMPv3 communication often requires access to both the manager and the agent logs, where detailed error messages can reveal whether authentication is failing, encryption keys are incorrect, or a user lacks the necessary permissions to access a specific OID.

Another frequent source of trouble is improper or incomplete MIB support. SNMP relies on MIBs to define the structure and semantics of the data being requested. If a device does not support a particular MIB module or if the manager does not have the correct MIB file loaded, the result may be unknown OIDs or unreadable data. This can happen when new hardware is introduced and its vendor-specific MIBs are not yet imported into the SNMP manager, or when different firmware versions change the set of supported MIB objects. Administrators may see generic OID numbers instead of meaningful labels, making it difficult to interpret the results. To resolve these issues, it is important to obtain and compile the appropriate MIB files for all monitored devices, ensuring they match the specific hardware and software versions in use.

SNMP traps present their own set of troubleshooting challenges. Since traps are unsolicited messages sent by devices to inform the manager of an event, ensuring their delivery requires that both the sender and receiver be correctly configured. A common mistake is failing to define the correct trap destination on the device. If the device sends traps to the wrong IP address, or if that address is unreachable, the manager will never receive them. Similarly, the SNMP manager must be listening on the correct interface and port to accept incoming trap messages. Firewalls and access control lists can also interfere with trap delivery. Unlike polling, which can be easily tested with tools like snmpget and snmpwalk, testing traps often requires triggering a real or simulated event, such as unplugging an interface or exceeding a CPU threshold. Monitoring tools may include utilities to simulate traps for testing purposes, allowing administrators to validate configuration without disrupting the production environment.

Timing and performance issues can also degrade SNMP functionality. In large networks with hundreds or thousands of devices, polling too frequently or requesting too much data at once can overwhelm devices or the management system. Symptoms may include missed polls, partial data collection, or timeouts. These problems can usually be mitigated by adjusting polling intervals, staggering poll times, or reducing the number of OIDs requested in a single query. SNMPv2c's GetBulk request can help reduce polling overhead, but only if devices support it and the manager is configured to take advantage of it. On the agent side, resource limitations can affect SNMP responsiveness. Some devices allocate minimal CPU or memory to SNMP processes, especially when under heavy operational load, which can result in delayed or dropped responses. Monitoring device health and system logs can help identify such performance bottlenecks.

Log files and debugging tools are invaluable in diagnosing SNMP problems. Many SNMP managers offer detailed logs of requests and responses, including timestamps, return codes, and error messages. Devices often provide debug or trace commands that show SNMP activity, which can be used to confirm whether queries are being received and how the agent is responding. SNMP packet capture using tools like Wireshark is another powerful technique for diagnosing low-level issues. By inspecting the actual SNMP packets exchanged between manager and agent, administrators can identify malformed requests, incorrect community strings, or cryptographic mismatches. These insights are especially useful in SNMPv3 environments, where encrypted traffic can obscure the true cause of communication failures unless both ends are properly aligned.

Maintaining documentation is another key component of troubleshooting. In environments with numerous devices and varying configurations, it is easy to lose track of which community strings, SNMP versions, or user credentials are in use. Keeping detailed records of SNMP configurations, including access control lists, user profiles, and MIB versions, helps streamline problem resolution and ensures consistency across the network. Regular audits and configuration reviews can also catch problems before they manifest as operational failures.

Ultimately, troubleshooting SNMP requires a blend of protocol knowledge, device familiarity, and systematic analysis. By approaching problems methodically—starting from basic connectivity and progressing through authentication, MIB resolution, trap handling, and performance tuning—administrators can isolate and resolve issues efficiently. Whether dealing with a simple switch that has stopped responding or a complex SNMPv3 authentication failure across dozens of routers, the troubleshooting process is grounded in understanding how each component of the SNMP system communicates and what dependencies it relies on. Through careful observation, testing, and validation, a reliable and secure SNMP environment can be maintained, ensuring that network operations remain transparent, predictable, and well-controlled.

Introduction to NetFlow Technology

NetFlow is a powerful and widely adopted network protocol developed by Cisco to collect and analyze IP traffic information as it enters or exits an interface on a network device. Since its introduction in the mid-1990s, NetFlow has become a standard method for obtaining deep visibility into network behavior, aiding in capacity planning, performance optimization, and security monitoring. At its core, NetFlow provides a structured and scalable way to observe the flow of data across a network, giving administrators a granular understanding of who is communicating, how much data is being exchanged, and over what time period. Unlike traditional SNMP-based monitoring, which focuses primarily on device and interface statistics, NetFlow operates at a higher layer of abstraction, allowing it to capture the context and patterns of actual traffic flows between endpoints.

The concept of a flow is central to how NetFlow operates. A flow is defined as a unidirectional sequence of packets sharing common characteristics, such as source and destination IP address, source and destination port, protocol type, type of service, and input interface. These fields are collectively known as the flow key. When a packet arrives at a NetFlow-enabled interface, the router or switch inspects the header and checks whether an existing flow record matches the characteristics of the packet. If a match is found, the counters for that flow are updated. If no match is found, a new flow record is created. This mechanism allows the device to summarize the details of thousands or millions of packets into a significantly smaller number of flow records, dramatically reducing the amount of data that must be processed and stored.

Once a flow has been created and its timeout conditions have been met—typically due to inactivity or flow completion—the flow record is exported from the device to a NetFlow collector. This collector is a server or appliance dedicated to receiving, storing, and analyzing NetFlow data. The export process involves encapsulating the flow records in UDP packets and transmitting them to the collector at regular intervals. These exported records include information such as the total number of bytes and packets observed, timestamps for the start and end of the flow, and any flags or counters associated with the traffic. Because this data is aggregated and lacks payload content, it provides an efficient and privacy-conscious way to gain insight into traffic behavior without the overhead of full packet capture.

NetFlow provides network administrators with an incredibly versatile toolset for understanding what is happening on their networks. By analyzing flow data, administrators can identify top talkers, detect unusual traffic patterns, locate bandwidth bottlenecks, and trace the path of specific communications. This level of insight is invaluable for both operational management and security monitoring. For example, during a distributed denial-of-service attack, NetFlow data can help pinpoint the source IP addresses generating excessive traffic, determine which destinations are being targeted, and assess the impact on the network. Likewise, in performance management scenarios, NetFlow can reveal underutilized links, overburdened interfaces, or application-specific traffic surges that require optimization or policy adjustments.

Another important benefit of NetFlow is its role in network capacity planning. By collecting long-term flow data, organizations can build detailed profiles of network usage over time. These profiles help in making informed decisions about upgrading infrastructure, adjusting traffic engineering policies, or reallocating bandwidth resources. Since NetFlow data includes timestamped information about traffic volume, it supports trend analysis and forecasting, enabling proactive planning rather than reactive troubleshooting. This capability is especially valuable in enterprise and service provider networks where bandwidth demands fluctuate based on user behavior, time of day, and application workloads.

NetFlow is also highly extensible and has evolved significantly since its original release. The first widely deployed version was NetFlow v5, which became a de facto standard and is still supported on many devices today. NetFlow v5 provides a fixed format and limited fields, but it remains suitable for many basic monitoring tasks. Later versions, such as NetFlow v9 and IPFIX (IP Flow Information Export), introduced template-based structures that allow for customizable flow records. These newer formats support the export of additional fields, such as MAC addresses, VLAN IDs, MPLS labels, and application identifiers. IPFIX, in particular, was developed as an IETF standard based on NetFlow v9 and is supported by a wide range of vendors, not just Cisco. This extensibility makes NetFlow adaptable to diverse network architectures, from simple LANs to complex multi-tenant data centers and cloud environments.

Deploying NetFlow typically involves configuring export parameters on routers or switches, including the destination collector IP address, the export version, and sampling options. Sampling is an important consideration in high-throughput networks, where capturing data for every single packet may be impractical. In such cases, administrators can configure statistical sampling techniques, such as 1 in every 100 packets, to reduce the volume of exported data while retaining a representative view of traffic flows. Sampling introduces a tradeoff between accuracy and performance, but when properly calibrated, it allows NetFlow to scale effectively across very large infrastructures.

Integration with analysis tools is another crucial aspect of a successful NetFlow deployment. Collectors and analysis platforms are responsible for processing and interpreting the raw flow data into meaningful visualizations and reports. These tools can identify anomalies, generate alerts, and support forensic investigations. Many modern network monitoring systems support NetFlow integration, offering dashboards that display bandwidth utilization, top applications, geolocation of traffic sources, and more. Some platforms even apply machine learning and behavioral analytics to flow data, detecting patterns that indicate security breaches or operational inefficiencies.

NetFlow plays a significant role in enhancing network security by enabling anomaly detection and traffic profiling. Because it tracks all traffic flows, it can reveal suspicious behavior, such as internal hosts communicating with known malicious IP addresses or unexpected data transfers to external networks. In environments where traditional signature-based intrusion detection systems may miss zero-day attacks or novel tactics, flow analysis provides an additional layer of defense. By continuously monitoring who is talking to whom, for how long, and over which protocols, NetFlow creates a baseline of normal behavior that can be used to flag deviations. These insights can be forwarded to SIEM systems or correlated with threat intelligence feeds to enrich the security response.

Organizations that rely on NetFlow benefit from improved operational awareness, faster incident response, and the ability to enforce and audit usage policies. Whether the goal is performance optimization, compliance enforcement, or threat detection, NetFlow offers a comprehensive and scalable approach to monitoring network traffic at a granular level. Its protocol-agnostic nature and extensive support across vendor platforms make it a valuable component of any network visibility strategy. As networks continue to evolve and adopt more distributed and dynamic architectures, the need for flow-based analysis tools like NetFlow will only become more pronounced, reinforcing its role as a foundational technology in modern network management.

NetFlow Versions and Their Differences

Since its initial development by Cisco in the 1990s, NetFlow has undergone significant evolution, resulting in several different versions that offer varying levels of functionality, flexibility, and compatibility. Each version of NetFlow was designed to address specific limitations or expand the scope of flow-based monitoring, adapting to the changing demands of network operations and technology. Understanding the differences between these versions is crucial for network administrators seeking to deploy NetFlow effectively across diverse infrastructures. While the core principle of exporting flow data remains consistent across versions, the structure of the exported records, supported features, and integration capabilities can vary significantly. The choice of version impacts not only the type of information collected but also the scalability, extensibility, and interoperability of the monitoring system as a whole.

The most widely known and deployed version of NetFlow is version 5. Introduced as a standard implementation for many Cisco devices, NetFlow v5 became the de facto baseline for flow monitoring across enterprise networks. It provided a fixed-format flow record that includes essential fields such as source and destination IP addresses, source and destination ports, protocol, type of service, input interface, number of packets, number of bytes, and timestamps for the start and end of the flow. This version was designed to meet the basic requirements of traffic accounting, bandwidth monitoring, and rudimentary network analysis. Because of its fixed structure, NetFlow v5 is easy to parse and process, which made it ideal for early flow collection tools. However, its limitations became more evident as network environments grew more complex. It lacked support for IPv6, did not include additional metadata like VLAN IDs or MAC addresses, and had no mechanism for extending the format to accommodate new data fields.

To address these limitations, Cisco introduced NetFlow version 7, a hardware-optimized variant that was only supported on specific platforms such as the Catalyst 6500 series with Supervisor Engine 2. NetFlow v7 added support for multipath data, allowing for more accurate representation of flows in networks using load balancing. However, like v5, it retained a fixed format and did not include extensibility. Its narrow platform support and incremental improvements meant that it was never widely adopted outside of specific high-performance scenarios. Version 7 is now largely obsolete and has been replaced by more flexible and robust solutions.

The real breakthrough in NetFlow came with version 9. NetFlow v9 introduced a template-based architecture, enabling variable-length flow records and supporting custom field definitions. This marked a significant departure from the rigid structures of earlier versions. Instead of a fixed set of fields, version 9 uses templates to define the structure of flow records, allowing for dynamic inclusion of additional information such as IPv6 addresses, MPLS labels, VLAN tags, next-hop IPs, and more. This flexibility made v9 suitable for monitoring modern, heterogeneous networks with advanced routing and tunneling

44

protocols. Templates are periodically exported alongside the flow records to ensure that collectors can accurately interpret the data being sent. This capability also paved the way for vendor-specific extensions and integration with application-aware network monitoring tools. NetFlow v9 became the foundation for the IP Flow Information Export protocol, or IPFIX, which was later standardized by the IETF.

IPFIX, often referred to as NetFlow version 10, builds on the concepts introduced in NetFlow v9 but extends them into a vendor-neutral, standards-based format. Unlike earlier versions that were proprietary to Cisco, IPFIX is an open standard designed to promote interoperability across different network equipment vendors. It preserves the template-based approach of v9 but allows for a much broader range of information elements, defined by IANA and extended by individual vendors as needed. IPFIX supports advanced features such as bidirectional flow correlation, variable-length strings, and enhanced time precision. It also permits transport over multiple protocols, including UDP, TCP, and SCTP, giving administrators greater control over reliability and performance. IPFIX has gained traction in multi-vendor environments and in scenarios where integration with security and analytics platforms is a priority.

One of the most important considerations when choosing between NetFlow versions is compatibility with both exporters and collectors. While many devices still support v5 due to its simplicity and low overhead, newer platforms increasingly default to v9 or IPFIX to take advantage of their extensibility and advanced features. Collectors must be capable of interpreting the version of NetFlow being used and, in the case of template-based formats, must dynamically adapt to the structure of each received flow record. Not all collectors support every version equally, and mismatches between exporter and collector capabilities can result in incomplete or unusable data. When deploying NetFlow in environments with mixed device types or newer traffic patterns such as IPv6, using v9 or IPFIX is often the better choice to ensure comprehensive coverage.

Another factor influencing the choice of NetFlow version is the specific use case or monitoring goal. For basic bandwidth utilization monitoring and traffic accounting, version 5 may be sufficient. Its lightweight structure reduces CPU and memory consumption on the exporting device and minimizes storage and processing requirements on the collector. For more complex tasks such as application performance monitoring, threat detection, or policy enforcement, the richer data available in v9 or IPFIX is essential. These versions enable visibility into traffic characteristics that cannot be captured by v5, such as Layer 2 information, application-layer identifiers, or encapsulation headers. They also support emerging technologies like network slicing and SD-WAN, where traditional flow metrics fall short.

Performance and scalability considerations also come into play when comparing NetFlow versions. While v5 generates less overhead and is suitable for high-throughput devices that require minimal impact on forwarding performance, v9 and IPFIX introduce additional complexity in template management and data parsing. Devices that support these versions typically have dedicated hardware or optimized software paths to handle flow export efficiently. Sampling techniques, such as probabilistic or deterministic sampling, can be employed to manage the volume of exported data, particularly in IPFIX deployments where very detailed records can produce large amounts of output.

NetFlow's evolution from v5 through to IPFIX reflects the growing demand for richer, more flexible, and vendor-agnostic network visibility solutions. Each version brings its own balance of simplicity, performance, extensibility, and interoperability. As networks continue to grow in size and complexity, the choice of NetFlow version will depend on the specific visibility requirements, the capabilities of the infrastructure, and the analytical goals of the organization. Understanding the differences between these versions ensures that network administrators can design monitoring systems that are not only efficient and scalable but also capable of adapting to future needs and emerging technologies.

Key Elements of a NetFlow Record

A NetFlow record represents a summarized snapshot of communication between two endpoints on a network. Rather than storing every individual packet, which can be overwhelming in both volume and detail, NetFlow records capture essential information about flows—groups of packets that share common characteristics. This efficiency allows administrators to analyze and understand traffic patterns without the need for full packet inspection. The data encapsulated in a NetFlow record provides invaluable insights into network behavior, including who is communicating, how often, how much data is exchanged, and when the communication occurs. Understanding the structure and key elements of a NetFlow record is essential for effectively deploying and leveraging flow-based network monitoring.

The foundation of a NetFlow record is the definition of a flow itself. A flow is determined by a set of attributes, often referred to as the seven-tuple in traditional NetFlow implementations. These include the source IP address, destination IP address, source port, destination port, layer 3 protocol type, type of service (ToS) byte, and the input interface. These attributes serve as the unique key that defines a specific flow. When a packet enters a NetFlow-enabled router or switch, the device examines the packet's header and determines whether it belongs to an existing flow or whether a new flow record must be created. If a match is found, counters in the existing flow are updated; if not, a new record is instantiated with initial values.

The source and destination IP addresses are fundamental elements in a flow record. They represent the origin and endpoint of the communication and are crucial for identifying traffic between users, services, and devices. By analyzing these addresses across many flows, administrators can determine which hosts generate the most traffic, identify unauthorized communication, or trace the path of specific sessions across the network. In environments with both IPv4 and IPv6, modern NetFlow versions such as v9 and IPFIX include fields for both types of addresses, allowing for comprehensive visibility regardless of IP version.

Source and destination ports provide the next layer of detail. While IP addresses identify the communicating endpoints, the ports specify the application or service associated with the flow. For example, port 80 usually indicates HTTP traffic, while port 443 suggests HTTPS. These fields allow administrators to classify flows based on application type, prioritize traffic, or detect unusual activity such as attempts to communicate on non-standard ports. In cases where applications use dynamic ports, correlating flows with known behaviors or additional context becomes necessary, but the port information remains an essential starting point for analysis.

The layer 3 protocol type, often represented by a numerical value, specifies whether the flow consists of TCP, UDP, ICMP, or another protocol. This information helps differentiate between connection-oriented and connectionless communication and assists in understanding the nature of traffic across the network. For instance, TCP traffic may suggest web browsing or file transfers, while ICMP may indicate network diagnostics or potential scanning activity. The protocol field enables filtering, categorization, and more refined analysis of traffic behavior.

Another key element in a NetFlow record is the type of service (ToS) byte, which reflects the quality of service parameters assigned to the flow. The ToS field, later expanded into the differentiated services code point (DSCP), provides insight into how the network is treating the flow in terms of priority, latency, and reliability. This is particularly important in environments where traffic is shaped or queued differently depending on its classification, such as in voice-over-IP (VoIP) or video streaming scenarios. By examining the ToS values in flow records, administrators can verify that QoS policies are being enforced correctly and troubleshoot issues related to latency-sensitive applications.

The input interface identifier, usually represented as a numerical index, indicates the physical or logical interface on the device where the flow was observed. This information is essential for understanding traffic directionality and determining where traffic enters or leaves the network. It also assists in capacity planning and device load monitoring. In more advanced flow records, an output interface index may also be included, providing a full picture of the forwarding path across the router or switch.

Flow counters are another critical component of NetFlow records. These include the total number of packets and the total number of bytes observed during the lifetime of the flow. These counters allow network teams to calculate throughput, monitor bandwidth consumption, and detect unusually large or small flows that might indicate file transfers or denial-of-service attacks. The ability to summarize this data across many flows supports high-level capacity analysis and long-term trend monitoring.

Timestamps for the start and end of the flow provide temporal context. These fields indicate when the flow began and when it ended, typically measured in milliseconds or microseconds from a reference point. Accurate timestamping is crucial for analyzing traffic behavior over time, correlating flow data with events from other sources like system logs or intrusion detection systems, and identifying patterns such as traffic bursts, application latency, or user activity trends. The precision and format of timestamps vary by NetFlow version, with newer formats offering finer granularity.

In NetFlow versions that support extensibility, additional elements can be included. These may consist of MAC addresses, VLAN identifiers, MPLS labels, autonomous system numbers, next-hop IP addresses, and exporter-specific metadata. Each of these fields enhances the visibility provided by the flow record and enables more detailed and context-rich analysis. For instance, VLAN IDs help distinguish traffic in multi-tenant environments, while MAC addresses can tie IP-level flows back to physical hardware in local area networks. Exporter and collector IPs also help trace where the data originated and which device reported the flow, which is essential in distributed monitoring architectures.

NetFlow v9 and IPFIX allow for vendor-specific extensions, making it possible to include proprietary metrics or custom-defined fields. These additions are often used to support application visibility, encrypted traffic fingerprinting, or integration with advanced security analytics platforms. The use of customizable templates in these versions means that organizations can tailor flow records to match their exact monitoring requirements, collecting only the data that is relevant to their operational goals.

The richness and diversity of information contained in a NetFlow record make it a powerful tool for network insight. Each field contributes to a comprehensive understanding of how data moves across the infrastructure. By analyzing flow records, administrators gain visibility into performance, security, capacity, and usage trends.

This allows them to optimize operations, detect anomalies, enforce policies, and respond quickly to emerging issues. Whether used in real-time dashboards or historical trend reports, the key elements of a NetFlow record serve as the foundation for intelligent, data-driven network management.

Configuring NetFlow on Cisco Devices

Implementing NetFlow on Cisco devices is a practical and effective way to gain insight into network traffic patterns, application usage, and bandwidth consumption. Cisco developed NetFlow as a technology embedded into its routers and switches to allow administrators to collect IP traffic information and export it to a centralized collector for analysis. Configuring NetFlow requires a combination of interface-level settings, global definitions, and exporter configurations. While the specific steps may vary slightly depending on the Cisco IOS version and hardware platform, the core process remains consistent across most environments. A proper configuration ensures accurate data collection, minimal performance impact, and seamless integration with NetFlow collectors or security analytics platforms.

The configuration process begins at the interface level, where traffic must be monitored and flow data must be collected. On most Cisco routers, NetFlow is enabled on a per-interface basis, and administrators must specify the direction of traffic to be monitored. The two primary options are ingress and egress. Ingress monitoring captures packets as they arrive at the interface, while egress monitoring captures packets as they leave. In many cases, ingress monitoring is sufficient and preferred due to its lower processing overhead and wider device compatibility. By applying NetFlow to both input and output directions, however, administrators can obtain a full picture of traffic patterns through each interface.

After enabling flow monitoring on the desired interfaces, the next step is to define the NetFlow exporter. The exporter is responsible for sending collected flow data from the device to a designated NetFlow collector. This involves specifying the collector's IP address, the transport protocol (typically UDP), and the destination port number used by the collector. The default port for NetFlow version 5 and version 9 is usually 2055, although other ports such as 9996 and 4739 are also commonly used, particularly for IPFIX. In this step, administrators can also set additional parameters such as source interface and export timers. The source interface defines which IP address the device will use as the source IP in NetFlow packets, which is critical for devices with multiple interfaces or in environments with strict access control policies.

Once the exporter is configured, it must be associated with a flow monitor. A flow monitor is a logical entity that ties together a record of the desired flow fields and the exporter that sends them. Flow monitors are defined globally and are applied to individual interfaces as needed. The flow monitor references a flow record, which defines the specific information to be captured for each flow. For basic traffic monitoring, Cisco provides predefined records, such as the NetFlow original record, which includes standard fields like IP addresses, ports, protocol type, and packet and byte counters. In more advanced configurations, custom flow records can be created to capture additional data such as VLAN IDs, MAC addresses, or MPLS labels.

Creating a custom flow record involves defining a set of match and collect statements. Match statements determine the criteria that group packets into flows, while collect statements specify which fields to include in the exported flow record. For example, an administrator might match on IPv4 source and destination addresses and collect byte counts, packet counts, and timestamps. Custom records allow greater flexibility and precision in data collection, especially in complex or multi-tenant environments where more granular visibility is required.

After defining the flow record and exporter, the flow monitor is created by binding the two together. The flow monitor must then be applied to the desired interface in either the input or output direction, depending on the traffic monitoring goals. This step activates NetFlow on the interface and begins the process of collecting flow data and exporting it to the collector. It is important to verify the configuration by checking the flow statistics on the device, which can reveal whether flows are being captured and exported correctly. Commands such as "show flow monitor" or "show ip cache flow" provide valuable real-time feedback on the operation of the NetFlow process.

For devices running older Cisco IOS versions or legacy platforms, NetFlow configuration may follow a simpler model using the command "ip flow ingress" or "ip route-cache flow" directly on interfaces. These commands automatically collect standard NetFlow data and export it to a globally defined collector. While this approach is less flexible than the modular configuration model introduced in Cisco IOS Flexible NetFlow, it is still widely used and effective in smaller or less complex environments. Regardless of the configuration method, it is essential to ensure that the device's CPU and memory resources are sufficient to handle the added load of flow monitoring, particularly on high-speed interfaces with large volumes of traffic.

To minimize performance impact, sampling can be configured. Sampling reduces the number of packets processed for flow analysis by selecting a representative subset. For example, a one-in-one-hundred sampling rate means only every hundredth packet is used to generate flow data. This technique significantly reduces the processing overhead on the device while still providing statistically meaningful information. Sampling is especially useful on interfaces with very high throughput or in scenarios where the volume of exported flow data must be constrained to conserve bandwidth or storage on the collector.

In addition to the technical configuration, administrators must also ensure that network policies and firewall rules allow NetFlow traffic to reach the collector. Since NetFlow exports are typically sent via UDP, they are susceptible to being blocked or dropped by firewalls, especially if unusual port numbers are used. Ensuring that appropriate access control entries are in place and that collector systems are properly configured to receive and parse flow data is essential to realizing the full benefits of a NetFlow deployment.

Configuring NetFlow on Cisco devices requires careful attention to detail, but once properly set up, it delivers a powerful window into network operations. Whether the goal is monitoring usage, enforcing policies, planning capacity, or enhancing security, NetFlow provides the data necessary to make informed decisions. The modular and flexible nature of Cisco's implementation allows administrators to tailor their configurations to fit a wide range of operational requirements. With thoughtful planning and correct implementation,

NetFlow becomes an indispensable tool for maintaining the health, performance, and security of modern networks.

Flow Exporters and Flow Collectors

The successful operation of any NetFlow-based monitoring system relies heavily on the interaction between flow exporters and flow collectors. These two components form the backbone of flow data analysis, working in tandem to provide a comprehensive and detailed view of network traffic. Flow exporters are responsible for capturing and packaging flow data from network devices, while flow collectors receive, store, and interpret that data. Each plays a unique and essential role in the NetFlow ecosystem, and the correct configuration and performance of both are vital for ensuring visibility, accuracy, and reliability in network monitoring operations.

A flow exporter resides on the network device, typically a router or switch, and is configured to observe traffic on one or more interfaces. When packets pass through the device, the exporter identifies flows based on predefined criteria such as source and destination IP addresses, ports, protocol, and other header fields. Each unique set of attributes defines a flow, and as packets matching the same attributes continue to arrive, the exporter maintains counters tracking the number of packets, bytes, and the timing of the flow. Rather than storing every packet, which would be highly inefficient, the exporter creates a summarized record of the flow. These records accumulate over time and are exported to the collector when the flow ends or reaches a timeout threshold. Exporters use a transport protocol such as UDP or, in more modern implementations, SCTP or TCP to transmit flow data to one or more designated collectors.

The configuration of flow exporters includes specifying which fields to collect, defining the export destination IP address, selecting the export protocol version, and determining export intervals or timeouts. In template-based versions like NetFlow v9 and IPFIX, exporters also send template records that describe the structure of the flow data. This allows the collector to understand and correctly parse the incoming information. Exporters must be configured with care to ensure that the correct level of detail is captured while balancing the processing and memory limitations of the device. Overloading a device with excessive flow tracking or overly frequent exports can lead to performance degradation, which is why sampling and selective flow monitoring are sometimes employed in high-throughput environments.

On the receiving end of the flow data is the flow collector. This component is typically a server or a dedicated appliance designed to receive, process, and store flow records from one or more exporters. The collector must be configured to listen on the correct port and accept traffic from the exporter's IP address. Upon receiving flow data, the collector decodes it using the appropriate templates, stores it in a database, and often feeds it into an analysis engine or visualization platform. Collectors can handle data from multiple exporters simultaneously, aggregating flows from various points across the network to provide a centralized view of traffic behavior.

Flow collectors are not just passive recipients of data. They play an active role in transforming raw flow records into meaningful information. By correlating flows over time, aggregating similar flows, and enriching flow data with external context such as DNS lookups, GeoIP information, or threat intelligence feeds, collectors become powerful tools for understanding network dynamics. Collectors also enable filtering, alerting, and reporting. For example, a collector might be configured to detect unusually high traffic from a single IP address, identify traffic that matches known malware signatures, or generate weekly usage summaries for bandwidth planning.

The architecture of a flow collection system can vary widely depending on the size and complexity of the network. In small environments, a single collector may be sufficient to handle all incoming data. In larger enterprise or service provider networks, multiple collectors may be deployed in a distributed architecture, often with hierarchical data aggregation or load balancing to ensure scalability and resilience. Some deployments also use intermediate concentrators that receive flow data from exporters and redistribute it to various collectors based on criteria such as traffic type, origin, or time period. This model supports flexible and fault-tolerant monitoring, especially when flow volumes are high or when data must be processed in parallel for different use cases.

Another important function of flow collectors is long-term storage and historical analysis. Unlike packet capture systems that may only store a short window of raw traffic due to storage limitations, flow collectors can retain summarized flow data for weeks, months, or even years. This historical visibility is invaluable for trend analysis, capacity planning, and forensic investigations. For example, when a security incident is discovered weeks after it occurred, flow records can help reconstruct the timeline of network activity, identify compromised systems, and reveal the extent of lateral movement or data exfiltration.

Security is a growing consideration in the configuration and operation of flow exporters and collectors. Because flow data can contain sensitive information about internal systems, communication patterns, and potential vulnerabilities, it is important to protect the flow export channel from unauthorized access or tampering. Using encrypted transport protocols, securing collectors behind firewalls, and authenticating access to flow data are common practices. Some implementations of IPFIX support secure export over TLS, offering enhanced protection for flow records in transit. Moreover, integrating flow collectors with security information and event management systems allows organizations to correlate flow data with other logs and alerts, enhancing their ability to detect and respond to threats.

Monitoring and maintaining flow exporter and collector performance is another critical aspect of a successful deployment. Exporters must be regularly checked to ensure that flows are being generated and exported without error. Collector logs should be monitored for dropped packets, decoding errors, or performance bottlenecks. Network time synchronization between exporters and collectors is also essential to ensure accurate timestamps, which are critical for correlating flow events and identifying traffic trends. Tools that visualize exporter performance and collector health can assist in managing these systems over time, ensuring they continue to deliver reliable and actionable insights.

Flow exporters and collectors are the operational pillars of NetFlow-based monitoring. Together, they enable the transformation of packet-level activity into high-level traffic intelligence. By understanding the role and configuration of each component, network administrators can design and implement flow monitoring systems that deliver the visibility and control required for modern network management. Whether the goal is traffic engineering, application performance monitoring, or security analytics, the seamless cooperation between flow exporters and flow collectors ensures that the right data is captured, interpreted, and made available for decision-making across the organization.

Analyzing Traffic with NetFlow

Analyzing traffic with NetFlow provides a deep and structured view of network behavior that goes far beyond simple interface statistics or device health indicators. NetFlow data enables administrators to observe how applications use bandwidth, identify which hosts are generating or receiving the most traffic, and recognize unusual patterns that may indicate performance problems or security threats. The core strength of NetFlow lies in its ability to summarize packet flows into metadata-rich records, which are then analyzed to extract meaningful insights about who is communicating, what services are being used, and how much data is exchanged over specific time intervals. This form of traffic analysis is both scalable and efficient, allowing for continuous monitoring without the storage and processing burdens of full packet capture.

When NetFlow records are collected from routers, switches, or firewalls, they are aggregated by flow collectors that transform the raw data into readable formats and feed it into analytical platforms. The process of traffic analysis begins with parsing these records into key dimensions such as source and destination IP addresses, source and destination ports, protocol types, and byte and packet counts. These basic elements serve as the foundation for identifying the relationships between devices and services on the network. For example, by sorting flow data by destination port, an administrator can determine how much traffic is being directed to common services like HTTP, HTTPS, DNS, or SMTP, and assess whether those usage levels are within expected norms.

Bandwidth analysis is one of the most common applications of NetFlow. By examining the total volume of traffic per IP address, subnet, or interface, administrators can detect congested links, bandwidth hogs, and inefficient routing. NetFlow allows this analysis to be done on a per-application or per-user basis, which is especially useful in environments where usage-based billing, departmental chargebacks, or application-level policy enforcement are necessary. Long-term storage of NetFlow records supports trend analysis, enabling comparisons of traffic usage across days, weeks, or months. This helps organizations plan for capacity upgrades, identify peak usage hours, and proactively address performance bottlenecks before they affect users.

Security monitoring is another powerful use case for NetFlow traffic analysis. Since NetFlow provides visibility into all flows, including those that may not trigger alarms in traditional intrusion detection systems, it plays a key role in detecting stealthy or anomalous activity. Suspicious traffic patterns such as port scanning, data exfiltration, and internal lateral movement often appear in NetFlow records as anomalies in traffic volume, destination diversity, or communication timing. For instance, a host that suddenly begins connecting to many different external IP addresses on random ports may be exhibiting behavior consistent with a botnet or worm infection. By establishing baselines of normal flow behavior, security teams can use NetFlow data to detect deviations in real time and take appropriate action.

Application usage analysis is further enhanced by classifying flows based on known port and protocol combinations. In some environments, deep packet inspection may be used in conjunction with NetFlow to refine application identification, especially for applications that use non-standard or dynamic ports. NetFlow analysis tools often incorporate application signatures to label traffic as belonging to specific categories such as video streaming, file sharing, cloud storage, or online gaming. This classification helps administrators enforce acceptable use policies, prioritize business-critical applications, and identify the root causes of performance degradation. In networks where application performance is tightly linked to business outcomes, such as in financial trading or healthcare, the ability to pinpoint slowdowns to specific flows is critical for maintaining service levels.

NetFlow also aids in identifying underutilized resources and inefficiencies. By correlating flow data with network topology, administrators can discover links that consistently operate below capacity or detect devices that receive very little traffic. This information can be used to optimize routing, redesign network segments, or reassign workloads to better distribute traffic. In virtualized and cloud environments, where traffic patterns can shift rapidly due to dynamic provisioning, NetFlow provides a stable and consistent mechanism for monitoring network usage even when the underlying infrastructure changes.

Geolocation and external threat intelligence can be integrated into NetFlow analysis to provide a richer context for external communications. By mapping source and destination IP addresses to geographic regions, analysts can detect unexpected or unauthorized data exchanges with foreign countries or suspicious IP ranges. When combined with threat intelligence feeds, NetFlow records can reveal communication with known malicious domains or command-and-control servers, enabling early detection of breaches. This context is especially important for compliance with regulatory requirements and for demonstrating due diligence in protecting sensitive information.

Visualization plays a significant role in making NetFlow traffic analysis accessible and actionable. Modern NetFlow tools present flow data through interactive dashboards, charts, and graphs that summarize key metrics such as top talkers, top applications, traffic trends, and alert conditions. These visualizations allow both technical and non-technical users to understand what is happening on the network at a glance. Drill-down capabilities enable detailed investigation of specific flows, hosts, or interfaces, facilitating root cause analysis and targeted troubleshooting. For instance, when users report slow application performance, administrators can use NetFlow analysis to quickly determine whether the problem is caused by local congestion, upstream provider issues, or application server bottlenecks.

Another important aspect of NetFlow traffic analysis is its role in supporting incident response and forensic investigation. When a security breach or service outage occurs, historical NetFlow data allows investigators to reconstruct the sequence of events, identify affected systems, and understand the scope of the incident. This retrospective capability is particularly valuable when logs are incomplete or when packet captures are not available. NetFlow data can reveal patterns that suggest credential abuse, rogue services, or data staging activity. By preserving NetFlow records over time, organizations gain the ability to answer critical questions long after an event has occurred.

NetFlow traffic analysis is not limited to reactive tasks. It also supports proactive network management strategies, such as anomaly detection, automated policy enforcement, and predictive analytics. Some platforms use machine learning to model normal flow behavior and generate alerts when deviations occur. Others can correlate NetFlow data with configuration management databases, ticketing systems, or user directories to automate workflows. As organizations continue to embrace software-defined networking and automation, NetFlow remains a foundational data source that supports intelligent decision-making and operational agility.

Analyzing traffic with NetFlow transforms raw packet metadata into actionable insights that support performance optimization, security enhancement, and strategic planning. By capturing the who, what, where, when, and how of network communication, NetFlow equips administrators with the visibility needed to manage increasingly complex and dynamic infrastructures. From identifying top consumers of bandwidth to uncovering hidden threats, the ability to analyze traffic through NetFlow provides a comprehensive and scalable approach to modern network monitoring.

Scalability Considerations in NetFlow

As networks grow in complexity and traffic volume, ensuring that NetFlow can scale to meet the demands of large and distributed infrastructures becomes a critical challenge. While NetFlow is a powerful and efficient method for collecting traffic metadata, its deployment across high-speed networks, multi-site environments, and data centers requires careful planning to avoid performance degradation, data loss, or operational bottlenecks. Scalability in NetFlow is not solely about supporting more devices or higher bandwidth. It involves managing the rate of flow generation, ensuring sufficient processing and storage capacity at the collection and analysis layers, and maintaining reliable transport of flow records from exporters to collectors. Each of these areas introduces potential limitations that must be addressed through architectural choices, protocol optimizations, and hardware tuning.

The first aspect of NetFlow scalability lies at the exporter level, where flow data is generated. Routers, switches, and firewalls must process large volumes of packets to identify unique flows, maintain counters, and periodically export records. On devices operating at gigabit or multi-gigabit speeds, the sheer number of flows per second can become overwhelming. Every TCP session, every burst of UDP traffic, and even short-lived connections contribute to the flow cache. If not managed properly, this can lead to cache overflows, increased CPU usage, and ultimately dropped flows. To prevent this, network administrators often employ sampling techniques, which reduce the number of packets analyzed for flow creation. For example, rather than analyzing every packet, a device might analyze one out of every 1,000. While this reduces accuracy, it significantly eases the processing burden and still provides statistically meaningful insights when the sample size is carefully chosen.

Another technique for managing exporter scalability involves tuning active and inactive flow timeouts. The active timeout defines the maximum duration a flow can remain in the cache before being exported, even if it is still ongoing. The inactive timeout determines how long the device will wait before expiring a flow that has not seen any new packets. Setting these timeouts appropriately is essential for balancing exporter performance with the granularity of flow data. Shorter timeouts result in more frequent exports, increasing load on the collector and network, while longer timeouts conserve resources but may delay visibility into fast-changing traffic patterns. The optimal timeout values depend on the nature of the traffic and the objectives of the monitoring effort.

Exporter hardware capabilities are also a limiting factor in scalability. Not all devices support the same NetFlow versions, and some platforms have hardware-accelerated flow processing, while others rely on software-based methods. Devices with limited memory or processing power may only support a small number of concurrent flows or a reduced feature set. In large-scale environments, it is essential to evaluate the flow export capabilities of each device and prioritize

NetFlow deployment on critical network segments. Where visibility is required on high-speed backbone links, devices with specialized flow hardware or dedicated flow processors should be selected to ensure reliable performance.

On the collection side, scalability concerns revolve around the ability to ingest, process, store, and analyze large volumes of flow records. Collectors must be able to handle thousands or even millions of flow records per second, depending on the network size. This requires not only high-performance storage and processing infrastructure but also efficient database and indexing strategies. Flow collectors that rely on relational databases may struggle under heavy loads unless carefully tuned. Many modern collectors use time-series databases or big data platforms to accommodate the high write rate and support rapid querying across large datasets. To support scalability, collectors may be deployed in distributed architectures with load balancers, redundant storage nodes, and horizontal scaling to handle increased throughput.

Network transport between exporters and collectors is another key area of concern. Since most NetFlow data is exported using UDP, there is no guaranteed delivery. In high-volume environments, flow data can be lost due to congestion, packet drops, or collector overload. To mitigate this, administrators can deploy multiple collectors and configure exporters with failover options. Using IPFIX or NetFlow v9 with TCP or SCTP transport can add reliability, although at the cost of increased overhead and complexity. Ensuring sufficient bandwidth and low latency between exporters and collectors is essential, particularly in geographically dispersed networks where data must cross WAN links. Compression and flow aggregation may be used to reduce the volume of exported data without sacrificing visibility.

Retention and historical analysis also present challenges at scale. Storing detailed flow data over long periods requires significant disk space, especially when monitoring hundreds of devices. Organizations must strike a balance between data granularity and retention duration. Some collectors support data rollups, where fine-grained data is retained for a short period and then aggregated into summaries for long-term storage. Others provide tiered storage strategies, moving older data to slower, less expensive storage media. These methods allow for efficient use of resources while preserving the ability to analyze trends, investigate incidents, and support compliance requirements.

Scalability in NetFlow also includes operational considerations. Managing configurations across many devices, ensuring synchronization of NetFlow templates, and maintaining consistency in flow formats are ongoing tasks. Automation tools and centralized configuration management systems can help streamline the deployment and monitoring of NetFlow across large environments. Integration with orchestration platforms and network controllers further simplifies the process, especially in software-defined networks or cloud-based infrastructures where devices are frequently added, removed, or reconfigured.

Visualization and reporting also require thoughtful design when working at scale. Dashboards must be able to handle large datasets and present meaningful insights without overwhelming users. Filtering and segmentation features are necessary to drill down into specific subsets of data, such as traffic for a particular department, application, or time window. Advanced analytics platforms may incorporate machine learning to automatically detect anomalies or suggest optimization strategies based on historical flow behavior. These capabilities rely on robust and scalable underlying data processing engines capable of handling the demands of enterprise-scale flow analysis.

Finally, security and privacy considerations must not be overlooked. With the growing importance of NetFlow in threat detection and compliance monitoring, the integrity and confidentiality of flow data become paramount. Large-scale deployments should include access controls, encryption, and audit trails to ensure that flow data remains trustworthy and protected. Scaling security alongside flow analysis ensures that visibility and compliance do not come at the expense of data exposure or operational risk.

Building a scalable NetFlow deployment is a multifaceted effort that requires attention to device capabilities, data transport, collector performance, storage strategies, and operational processes. Each layer must be designed to handle not just current traffic levels but also future growth. By approaching NetFlow with scalability in mind from the outset, organizations can ensure that they maintain comprehensive and actionable visibility into their networks as they expand and evolve.

NetFlow Security Implications

NetFlow, as a powerful technology for collecting and analyzing IP traffic data, provides exceptional visibility into the operational behavior of a network. It enables administrators to track conversations, detect anomalies, and profile network usage with precision. However, as with any monitoring system that gathers sensitive information, NetFlow itself introduces important security implications. These implications span across data privacy, infrastructure exposure, misuse by threat actors, and integration with broader security frameworks. A comprehensive understanding of these aspects is essential for deploying NetFlow securely, ensuring that while it enhances security and operations, it does not inadvertently create new vulnerabilities.

One of the most significant security concerns with NetFlow is the potential exposure of metadata that can reveal detailed information about internal network activity. While NetFlow does not capture payloads or user credentials, it does log who is talking to whom, on what ports, using which protocols, and for how long. This metadata is highly valuable not only for network operations but also for attackers conducting reconnaissance. If NetFlow export traffic is intercepted or collected by unauthorized parties, it can be used to map the network topology, identify high-value targets, detect security gaps, and plan lateral movement. For example, observing a high volume of traffic from a particular host to a server on port 389 might suggest LDAP activity, revealing an identity infrastructure component that could be exploited. Therefore, NetFlow data should be treated with the same care as other forms of sensitive telemetry, and access must be tightly controlled.

The transport of NetFlow data from exporters to collectors is often done using the UDP protocol, which does not provide encryption, authentication, or delivery guarantees. This exposes NetFlow traffic to potential eavesdropping, tampering, and packet loss, especially if it traverses untrusted or public network segments. Attackers positioned between exporters and collectors could sniff flow records in transit, gaining real-time visibility into internal communications. In more sophisticated attacks, they could inject forged NetFlow data to mislead analysis systems, masking real attacks or causing false alarms. To mitigate these risks, administrators should isolate NetFlow traffic on dedicated management networks or VPN tunnels and use versions of NetFlow or IPFIX that support encrypted transport mechanisms like TLS or DTLS when available.

Another consideration is the possibility of NetFlow collectors themselves becoming targets of attack. These systems accumulate and store large volumes of network data and are often integrated into broader analytics platforms and security information and event management solutions. If compromised, a collector could provide attackers with historical insights into the network, allow tampering with traffic analysis outcomes, or become a launchpad for further attacks. Therefore, collectors must be hardened following best security practices, including strict access controls, patch management, log monitoring, and segmentation from general-purpose user networks. Role-based access should be enforced on flow analysis platforms to ensure that only authorized personnel can view or manipulate flow data. Some organizations may also opt to hash or anonymize parts of the flow record, such as internal IP addresses, before long-term storage or external sharing, in order to reduce data sensitivity.

Beyond protecting the NetFlow infrastructure, another security implication arises from the misuse of NetFlow itself as a reconnaissance tool by malicious insiders or compromised systems. Since flow data can be used to infer the structure and behavior of the network, unauthorized use of NetFlow queries or exports could enable internal reconnaissance efforts that precede privilege escalation or data exfiltration. Monitoring the configuration of NetFlow on all devices is essential to ensure that only intended interfaces are exporting flows and only to designated collectors. Configuration audits should be performed regularly to detect deviations or anomalies. Logging changes to NetFlow-related configurations provides an audit trail that is helpful for compliance and incident investigation.

The insights provided by NetFlow also present opportunities for enhancing network security when used correctly. Flow data can be used to detect command and control communications, unusual port usage, sudden traffic spikes, or the spread of malware within the internal network. By establishing baselines of expected flow behavior, organizations can implement behavior-based detection models that identify anomalies with high fidelity. Integrating NetFlow with intrusion detection systems, threat intelligence platforms, and SIEM tools allows for more accurate alerting and incident correlation. For instance, a security event indicating a possible compromise can be correlated with NetFlow data to determine which systems communicated with the affected host before and after the event, providing immediate leads for further investigation.

It is important to consider the regulatory and compliance context in which NetFlow data is collected and stored. Regulations such as GDPR, HIPAA, or PCI-DSS may apply depending on the nature of the data being processed and the geography in which the organization operates. While NetFlow does not usually include personally identifiable information or content, when correlated with other data sources, it can contribute to identifying individuals or behaviors. This risk makes it necessary to assess the retention policies, data access controls, and anonymization practices applied to flow data. Transparent documentation and privacy impact assessments may be required to ensure that NetFlow usage aligns with organizational policies and legal obligations.

Scalability and volume also affect the security implications of NetFlow. In large environments, managing the sheer quantity of flow data can become a challenge, and the possibility of data overload or blind spots increases. An overburdened collector or an improperly tuned analysis system may fail to detect critical events buried in massive datasets. Security teams must balance the granularity of flow data with the ability to process and interpret it meaningfully. Sampling, aggregation, and filtering mechanisms can reduce noise while preserving the visibility needed for security monitoring. However, these techniques must be applied with care to avoid inadvertently omitting essential indicators of compromise or early signs of attack.

Finally, awareness and training are crucial for ensuring that NetFlow is used securely and effectively. Security and network operations teams must be familiar with the potential risks and benefits of flow monitoring. Clear policies should define who has access to NetFlow data, how it is to be used, and under what circumstances data sharing with third parties is permissible. Collaboration between security, compliance, and network engineering teams ensures that NetFlow deployments are aligned with broader organizational goals and risk management strategies.

NetFlow, when properly secured and integrated into a comprehensive monitoring and analytics framework, becomes an indispensable tool in the defense and operation of modern networks. The very characteristics that make it valuable for insight and detection also make it a sensitive asset that requires protection. By understanding and addressing the security implications of NetFlow, organizations can harness its full potential while maintaining the integrity, confidentiality, and reliability of their monitoring infrastructure.

Use Cases for NetFlow in Enterprise Networks

NetFlow is an indispensable tool in enterprise networks, offering a wealth of information that enhances visibility, security, performance management, and operational efficiency. Its ability to collect metadata about IP traffic and provide detailed insights into how data flows across the network allows enterprises to address a wide range of challenges that span both the technical and business domains. NetFlow does not rely on full packet inspection, making it a scalable and efficient method for continuous monitoring across diverse environments. The value it provides to enterprises lies not only in the raw data it captures but in the variety of strategic use cases it supports.

One of the most prominent use cases for NetFlow in enterprise networks is traffic analysis. Enterprises must understand how their network is being used, who the top consumers are, what applications are driving bandwidth consumption, and where potential congestion points exist. By analyzing NetFlow records, IT teams can break down traffic by source and destination IPs, port numbers, and protocol types, gaining insights into which services are operating at high capacity and whether they align with business-critical applications. For example, an administrator might discover that video conferencing traffic has spiked during work hours, requiring policy changes to ensure adequate bandwidth allocation for voice and collaboration tools. Alternatively, discovering that large volumes of traffic are generated by unauthorized applications can lead to adjustments in firewall rules or user education initiatives.

Capacity planning and bandwidth forecasting also benefit significantly from NetFlow data. As enterprises grow, so do their network demands. Having historical traffic records helps IT planners anticipate future growth and make informed decisions about upgrading links, deploying new hardware, or reallocating bandwidth resources. Trends derived from NetFlow data can highlight peak usage times, persistent underutilization of certain network segments, or the gradual increase in usage by specific departments or services. This proactive planning approach reduces the risk of outages or performance bottlenecks and supports budgeting processes with concrete data.

NetFlow is also an invaluable asset for enhancing security posture within the enterprise. Traditional security systems often focus on perimeter defense or endpoint protection, but many threats originate or propagate internally. With NetFlow, security teams can monitor east-west traffic between internal systems, detecting anomalies such as lateral movement, port scanning, or unexpected data exfiltration attempts. A compromised host may begin communicating with multiple unknown external IP addresses on uncommon ports, a behavior that NetFlow can reveal quickly. Flow-based anomaly detection, often integrated into security information and event management systems, allows enterprises to detect threats that evade traditional signature-based systems. By correlating NetFlow with threat intelligence feeds, organizations can identify and respond to attacks in earlier stages of the kill chain.

Incident response and forensic analysis also rely heavily on NetFlow. When a security incident occurs, having a complete and timestamped record of all network flows enables investigators to reconstruct the timeline, identify affected systems, and determine how the attacker moved through the network. NetFlow provides a historical footprint that persists even when other logs are missing or incomplete. Forensics teams can use this data to identify the initial point of compromise, track data transfers to external sites, and assess the scope of the breach. This level of visibility is essential for post-incident reporting, compliance requirements, and improving future defenses.

In large enterprises with multiple locations or business units, NetFlow also supports multi-tenant network visibility. Different departments may operate semi-independently but share common infrastructure. NetFlow allows administrators to segment traffic logically, track interdepartmental communications, and enforce usage policies. In cases where chargeback models are used, NetFlow provides accurate data for billing departments or business units based on actual resource consumption. By tying flow data to user identities or organizational roles, enterprises can implement detailed and auditable access and usage policies, aligning IT operations with business governance frameworks.

Application performance monitoring is another domain where NetFlow plays a critical role. Modern enterprises rely on cloud services, SaaS platforms, and distributed applications that span multiple sites and data centers. NetFlow helps measure how well these applications perform by capturing latency metrics, flow duration, and round-trip communication patterns. When users report slow response times or application failures, administrators can use NetFlow to determine if the issue lies in the network, the server, or an external dependency. This enables faster root cause identification and minimizes downtime. NetFlow's ability to track traffic across WAN links, VPN tunnels, and hybrid environments gives administrators the end-to-end visibility they need to ensure consistent application delivery.

Regulatory compliance is yet another area where NetFlow supports enterprise operations. Industries such as finance, healthcare, and government are subject to strict regulations regarding data handling, access control, and breach reporting. NetFlow provides a passive yet powerful means of logging all communication across the network. This helps demonstrate due diligence in securing sensitive data, detecting policy violations, and auditing access to critical systems. Regulatory frameworks often require visibility into data flows and network activity, and NetFlow fills this need without the complexity or overhead of intrusive packet inspection. Furthermore, long-term flow data storage enables retrospective audits and satisfies retention requirements imposed by legal or contractual obligations.

NetFlow is also used in validating and optimizing network segmentation, which is a key strategy in enterprise cybersecurity. Organizations implement segmentation to isolate sensitive data and reduce the blast radius of potential attacks. By monitoring flow records, administrators can confirm whether segmentation policies are working as intended. If unexpected flows are observed between isolated segments, this indicates a misconfiguration or policy violation. This feedback loop allows for the continuous refinement of network access controls and ensures that internal security zones remain effective.

Another practical use case involves supporting network migrations and infrastructure changes. During major transitions such as data center relocations, cloud adoption, or the rollout of new services, it is critical to understand existing traffic flows to avoid disrupting operations. NetFlow helps identify dependencies between systems, traffic volumes between locations, and the timing of critical transactions. Armed with this information, IT teams can plan migrations more accurately, test fallback scenarios, and verify that performance levels remain acceptable after changes are made.

In addition to its technical benefits, NetFlow supports strategic decision-making at the organizational level. The data collected from NetFlow can be translated into executive dashboards that highlight key performance indicators, service availability, and compliance status. By visualizing network behavior in terms that align with business goals, NetFlow becomes not only a tool for engineers but a source of insight for decision-makers. It bridges the gap between technical operations and business outcomes, demonstrating the value of IT investments and the effectiveness of risk management strategies.

NetFlow continues to be one of the most versatile tools available to enterprise network teams. Its ability to provide high-fidelity traffic visibility without overwhelming the network or storage infrastructure makes it uniquely positioned to support a wide range of operational, security, and compliance use cases. By leveraging NetFlow in these varied contexts, enterprises can build smarter, safer, and more responsive networks that align with their evolving digital strategies.

Introduction to sFlow Monitoring

sFlow is a network traffic monitoring technology designed to provide visibility into data flows across high-performance networks. Unlike traditional packet capture tools or polling-based systems like SNMP, sFlow offers a scalable and efficient method to monitor network activity in real time. It operates by capturing a statistical sample of traffic flowing through network devices and exporting this information to a centralized collector for analysis. sFlow has gained popularity in environments where high throughput and scalability are required, such as data centers, service provider networks, and enterprise backbones. Its lightweight design and minimal impact on device performance make it a preferred choice for monitoring large volumes of traffic without introducing latency or consuming excessive resources.

The concept behind sFlow is rooted in sampling. Instead of inspecting every packet or maintaining detailed state information about every flow, sFlow uses probabilistic techniques to select representative packets and periodically collects counter data from monitored interfaces. These samples are encapsulated in sFlow datagrams and exported via UDP to a collector, where they are processed and analyzed. The sampling process ensures that the monitoring burden on network devices is kept very low, making sFlow particularly suitable for high-speed links and densely populated switches. This sampling method provides a statistically accurate picture of network usage while remaining scalable across thousands of ports and terabits of throughput.

One of the distinguishing features of sFlow is its vendor-neutral design. It is defined by the sFlow.org specification and supported by a wide range of networking vendors, including Arista, Juniper, Brocade, HPE, and many others. This broad support allows organizations to implement sFlow in multi-vendor environments without relying on proprietary extensions or specialized hardware. The standardization of sFlow ensures consistency in data export formats, making integration with third-party analysis tools and centralized monitoring platforms straightforward. Furthermore, its ability to capture both Layer 2 and Layer 3 data provides a more holistic view of network behavior, including insights into VLAN usage, MAC address activity, and protocol distribution.

The sFlow architecture consists of three primary components: the sFlow agent, the sFlow collector, and the network management application. The sFlow agent is typically embedded in the firmware of switches and routers. It is responsible for selecting samples, constructing sFlow datagrams, and sending them to the collector. The agent can be configured to define the sampling rate, which determines how frequently packets are sampled. For instance, a sampling rate of 1:1000 means that on average, one out of every 1,000 packets is selected for export. The agent also collects interface counters, such as the number of bytes and packets sent or received, and includes this information in its reports. These counters complement the packet samples by providing traffic volume statistics that are essential for bandwidth analysis and capacity planning.

The sFlow collector receives datagrams from multiple agents, decodes the information, and stores it for further processing. The collector can correlate the samples with network topology data, perform traffic analysis, and present the results in visual dashboards or generate alerts. Advanced collectors may also enrich the data with contextual information, such as hostnames, application identification, or geolocation of IP addresses. The collector acts as the central point for aggregating and analyzing network data, enabling both real-time and historical insights into traffic behavior. By analyzing patterns over time, the collector helps identify trends, detect anomalies, and optimize network performance.

A key advantage of sFlow is its ability to monitor all traffic types, including unicast, multicast, and broadcast, as well as control plane and management traffic. This universal visibility allows administrators to gain a comprehensive understanding of how network resources are being utilized. sFlow is especially effective in detecting microbursts, packet drops, and congestion events that might not be visible through SNMP polling. Because sFlow samples packets as they are forwarded, it captures transient events that could otherwise go unnoticed. This makes it a valuable tool for troubleshooting performance issues, validating quality of service policies, and verifying network segmentation.

Another important use of sFlow is in security monitoring. Packet samples provide rich metadata about communication sessions, including source and destination addresses, ports, and protocol types. This information can be used to detect suspicious behavior, such as scanning activity, denial-of-service attacks, or data exfiltration. By establishing baselines for normal traffic patterns, security teams can use sFlow to identify anomalies that may indicate compromise. Unlike deep packet inspection, which is resource-intensive and may violate privacy regulations, sFlow offers a balance between visibility and efficiency, capturing enough data to detect threats without exposing payloads or overwhelming the monitoring infrastructure.

sFlow also plays a critical role in software-defined networking and dynamic environments. As networks become increasingly virtualized and programmatically controlled, the need for real-time telemetry that scales with changing topologies grows. sFlow fits well into these environments due to its stateless nature and low overhead. It can monitor traffic in both physical and virtual environments, including virtual switches and overlay networks. With the ability to export data continuously, sFlow enables feedback loops that support automation, self-healing networks, and intent-based networking models. Administrators can programmatically adjust policies or traffic paths based on real-time insights provided by sFlow, leading to more responsive and resilient network operations.

From a deployment perspective, configuring sFlow is generally straightforward. Administrators specify the collector IP address, the UDP port for export, the sampling rate, and polling intervals for counters. Most devices allow these parameters to be set on a per-interface basis, allowing for flexible and targeted monitoring. For example, high-value interfaces such as uplinks or WAN connections may be configured with lower sampling rates for higher accuracy, while edge interfaces may use higher rates to reduce overhead. The simplicity of the configuration and the minimal processing load make sFlow an attractive option for organizations looking to extend visibility without extensive infrastructure upgrades.

Despite its strengths, sFlow does require careful consideration in terms of data interpretation. Since it relies on sampling, there is an inherent trade-off between data volume and accuracy. While statistical methods can extrapolate accurate results from sampled data, high granularity is not always achievable, particularly for very short-lived flows or low-volume traffic. Organizations must choose sampling rates that strike the right balance between resource efficiency and visibility. Collectors and analysis tools must also be able to properly account for the sampling ratio when generating reports to avoid misrepresentation of traffic volumes or flow counts.

sFlow provides an effective, scalable, and vendor-agnostic approach to network traffic monitoring. Its sampling-based methodology allows it to operate efficiently in high-speed environments, delivering real-time insights into network performance, application behavior, and security events. With widespread industry support, ease of deployment, and compatibility with modern network architectures, sFlow continues to be a valuable asset for network administrators and architects seeking to maintain visibility and control in today's increasingly dynamic and high-throughput environments.

Comparing sFlow and NetFlow

When examining modern approaches to network visibility and traffic monitoring, sFlow and NetFlow emerge as two of the most prominent protocols, each with distinct characteristics, strengths, and deployment considerations. Although both are designed to provide insights into network usage, application behavior, and traffic patterns, the methodologies they use to achieve these goals are fundamentally different. Understanding the comparative nature of sFlow and NetFlow is essential for network architects and administrators when selecting a protocol that aligns with the needs of their infrastructure, performance objectives, and operational strategies.

At the core of their difference lies the way they collect and export data. NetFlow is a flow-based protocol that records conversations between endpoints by aggregating packets into flows based on shared attributes such as source and destination IP address, port numbers, protocol, and type of service. A flow begins when a unique set of these attributes is first observed and ends when it expires, either due to inactivity or reaching a timeout. During its lifetime, a flow record accumulates statistics like packet and byte counts, timestamps, and interface identifiers. These flow records are then periodically exported to a collector. In contrast, sFlow takes a sampling approach, capturing packet headers and interface counters at specified intervals and rates. Rather than maintaining state about flows, sFlow samples one out of every N packets based on a configured rate and sends the captured data immediately to the collector without waiting for flow completion.

The practical result of this difference is that NetFlow provides complete flow data for all observed traffic when configured to do so, making it ideal for environments where detailed, per-session information is needed. However, this comes at the cost of higher resource consumption on the exporting devices, especially in high-throughput networks with large numbers of concurrent flows. Maintaining flow caches and exporting records can place significant demands on CPU and memory, particularly when using NetFlow on devices that lack hardware acceleration. sFlow, by design, avoids this issue by reducing the volume of data it must handle. Since it only samples a subset of traffic, it imposes minimal overhead on devices and scales efficiently even on links operating at tens or hundreds of gigabits per second.

The sampling method used by sFlow can lead to less precise measurements for very short-lived flows or low-volume communications, particularly if the sampling rate is not aggressive enough. On the other hand, NetFlow provides higher granularity and accuracy, particularly for analyzing session behavior, timing characteristics, or application usage. This makes NetFlow more suitable for forensic investigations, detailed application performance monitoring, and compliance audits where exact traffic records may be required. In environments where every session counts, such as financial trading networks or security-sensitive infrastructure, NetFlow's detail-oriented approach is often preferred.

From a vendor support perspective, NetFlow originated with Cisco and was initially implemented in a proprietary format, although newer versions such as NetFlow version 9 and IPFIX have opened the door to extensibility and broader vendor adoption. sFlow, in contrast, was developed as a vendor-neutral standard under the guidance of the sFlow.org consortium, and it is natively supported by a wide variety of networking vendors. This makes sFlow particularly attractive in multi-vendor environments where consistency and interoperability are important considerations. Additionally, because sFlow is stateless and its export format is consistent across implementations, it tends to be easier to parse and analyze with open-source and commercial collectors.

Another key comparison lies in how these protocols interact with different network types and topologies. NetFlow is most commonly deployed on routers and Layer 3 switches, as its design focuses on IP traffic and flow aggregation. While it can also be used on Layer 2 devices that support it, its strengths lie in environments where routed traffic and protocol identification are central to the monitoring goals. sFlow, with its capability to monitor both Layer 2 and Layer 3 traffic, is better suited for deployment in data centers and switching fabrics where MAC address visibility, VLAN monitoring, and traffic mirroring are important. It offers broader coverage in environments where Layer 2 plays a significant operational role.

When considering security monitoring, both protocols offer valuable insights but approach detection differently. NetFlow's detailed flow records are beneficial for identifying anomalies in communication behavior, such as data exfiltration attempts, unusual lateral movement, or command and control communications. The full flow context provides the ability to reconstruct sessions and trace the sequence of events with high confidence. sFlow, while lacking full flow visibility, offers a continuous stream of sampled packets, which can capture a wide range of communication patterns across the network. This makes it effective for detecting large-scale anomalies, such as DDoS attacks, scanning activity, or bandwidth abuse. The ability to see every part of the network, including control plane traffic, enhances sFlow's role in real-time threat detection and response.

From an operational perspective, deploying and managing sFlow is generally simpler and less resource-intensive. Configuring sampling rates and defining collectors is typically all that is required, and most network devices that support sFlow do so with minimal performance impact. NetFlow configurations can be more complex, particularly when dealing with flexible NetFlow, where flow records, exporters, and monitors must be defined and applied to interfaces. Additionally, NetFlow deployments often require careful tuning of timeouts and export intervals to balance visibility with performance and to prevent overwhelming the collector with excessive data.

Storage and analysis also present a contrast. Since NetFlow can generate large volumes of detailed flow records, collectors must be designed to handle high write rates and maintain large datasets. This often necessitates high-performance storage systems and efficient indexing strategies. sFlow, due to its sampled nature, generates less data and is therefore easier to manage and analyze, particularly in environments where storage capacity is constrained or where rapid data processing is required. However, interpreting sFlow data accurately requires careful attention to statistical principles and understanding the implications of the configured sampling rates.

Both protocols have found their niche in enterprise and service provider networks, often being used in complementary ways. For example, NetFlow may be deployed at key network chokepoints to capture detailed records for security audits and troubleshooting, while sFlow provides broad, low-overhead visibility across switching fabrics and access layers. Together, they offer a comprehensive monitoring strategy that balances depth with scalability. The choice between sFlow and NetFlow ultimately depends on the specific goals of the monitoring initiative, the architecture of the network, and the performance characteristics of the hardware involved.

By evaluating the nature of traffic, the desired level of visibility, and the operational constraints of the environment, network teams can determine which protocol offers the best fit. Both sFlow and NetFlow represent mature and powerful solutions for gaining control and insight into complex network infrastructures, and understanding their respective capabilities allows organizations to build monitoring systems that are both robust and adaptable.

Flow Agent and Collector Design

The architecture of flow monitoring systems relies fundamentally on the interaction between flow agents and flow collectors. These two components form the backbone of protocols like NetFlow, sFlow, and IPFIX, serving as the origin and destination of flow data, respectively. Designing flow agents and collectors involves several critical considerations that influence the accuracy, performance, and scalability of the overall monitoring infrastructure. When implemented correctly, they enable real-time visibility into network activity, support forensic analysis, provide data for capacity planning, and enhance security monitoring. The challenge lies in ensuring that both the agent and the collector can efficiently handle the volume, variety, and velocity of flow data typical of modern high-speed networks.

A flow agent is typically a software or firmware component embedded in a network device such as a router, switch, or firewall. Its core function is to observe traffic as it passes through the device and generate flow records based on defined criteria. For NetFlow, this involves inspecting packet headers and aggregating packets that share common attributes into flow entries. These entries are stored temporarily in a flow cache, which maintains statistics such as the number of packets, total bytes, flow start time, and end time. When a flow expires due to timeout or completion, the agent exports the flow record to a collector. In contrast, sFlow agents use a sampling approach, where the agent selects one out of every N packets for export, along with periodic counter data, without maintaining state about flows.

The efficiency and effectiveness of a flow agent depend heavily on the design of its flow cache and the granularity of its sampling or aggregation mechanisms. The cache must be large enough to store a sufficient number of concurrent flows, especially in environments with heavy or bursty traffic. If the cache overflows, older or inactive flows may be prematurely evicted, resulting in lost visibility and incomplete records. High-performance agents implement cache aging algorithms and configurable timeouts to balance memory usage with data fidelity.

Sampling rates must be carefully selected to provide representative data while minimizing the processing load. For sFlow agents, which sample packets rather than flows, the packet selection mechanism must ensure randomness and uniformity to maintain statistical validity.

Another key aspect of flow agent design is the ability to customize which fields are collected and exported. Flexible flow definitions allow administrators to tailor data collection to specific use cases. In NetFlow version 9 and IPFIX, templates define the structure of exported flow records, enabling the inclusion of additional fields such as VLAN IDs, MAC addresses, MPLS labels, application identifiers, and next-hop information. Advanced agents support dynamic template generation and export to adapt to different network segments and monitoring requirements. The flexibility to include or exclude specific fields reduces bandwidth usage and processing demands while ensuring that the most relevant data is collected.

Security is also a critical factor in flow agent design. Since flow data can reveal sensitive information about internal systems and communication patterns, agents must protect against unauthorized access and manipulation. This includes limiting the IP addresses to which flow data can be sent, enforcing export authentication where supported, and ensuring that the agent process is not vulnerable to attacks that could disable monitoring or corrupt data. Agents embedded in network devices must also coexist peacefully with other processes, avoiding excessive resource consumption that could impact packet forwarding or routing performance.

On the receiving side, the flow collector is responsible for ingesting flow data, decoding it, storing it, and making it available for analysis. A well-designed collector must be able to handle high volumes of flow records per second, maintain data integrity, and scale horizontally as monitoring demands increase. Collectors typically consist of multiple components, including input handlers to receive data from the network, decoders to parse protocol-specific fields, storage engines to persist flow records, and analytics modules to interpret and visualize data. The input handler must support the transport protocols used by agents, typically UDP for NetFlow and sFlow, and optionally TCP or SCTP for IPFIX. Since UDP is connectionless and does not guarantee delivery, collectors must be resilient to packet loss and capable of handling out-of-order or incomplete flow records.

Storage is one of the most demanding aspects of collector design. Flow data is high in volume but lower in entropy compared to full packet captures. Nevertheless, the collector must efficiently index and compress flow records to allow rapid retrieval and long-term retention. Time-series databases, NoSQL platforms, or custom-built storage engines are often used to meet these needs. The storage architecture must support high write throughput while maintaining query performance for dashboards, reports, and alerts. Data retention policies determine how long detailed flow records are kept and whether they are aggregated or archived over time. Compression techniques and roll-up mechanisms help reduce storage costs without compromising analytical value.

Analytics modules in a flow collector transform raw data into actionable insights. This includes aggregating flows by host, application, or geography, detecting anomalies, identifying top talkers, and correlating flow data with other sources like DNS, DHCP, and threat intelligence feeds. Advanced collectors support machine learning algorithms that learn normal network behavior and trigger alerts on deviations. Dashboards and visualization tools present data in user-friendly formats, allowing both technical and non-technical stakeholders to monitor network health and performance.

Scalability and fault tolerance are vital in enterprise and service provider environments. Flow collectors must be able to process data from hundreds or thousands of devices without becoming a bottleneck. Load balancing, sharding, and clustering techniques distribute the workload across multiple servers. High availability configurations ensure that data is not lost during hardware failures or software upgrades. Monitoring tools track the health of collector components and provide alerts if data ingestion slows, storage approaches capacity, or resource utilization becomes excessive.

Flow agent and collector design must also consider integration with broader IT and security ecosystems. APIs and connectors allow flow data to feed into SIEM platforms, cloud monitoring tools, and automation systems. Standardized export formats and schemas facilitate compatibility and data normalization. As network environments evolve to include hybrid clouds, containers, and virtualized workloads, agents and collectors must adapt by supporting virtual deployments, cloud-native telemetry sources, and elastic scaling models.

Designing effective flow agents and collectors is about more than just technical specifications. It requires a deep understanding of network behavior, operational goals, and the trade-offs between visibility, performance, and cost. By focusing on efficiency, flexibility, security, and scalability, organizations can build monitoring infrastructures that not only support current needs but are ready to grow with the demands of future technologies and network architectures. The coordination between intelligent agents at the edge and robust collectors at the core ensures that flow monitoring remains a reliable and powerful tool for network management and security analytics.

Flow Sampling Techniques and Accuracy

Flow sampling is a critical technique in scalable network traffic monitoring, particularly in high-speed and high-density environments where analyzing every single packet would overwhelm system resources. Instead of capturing every packet or generating flow records for every communication session, flow sampling reduces the data volume by selecting a representative subset of packets or flows based on predefined sampling methods. This approach ensures that network devices can monitor traffic efficiently without compromising their primary performance responsibilities. However, the accuracy of monitoring outcomes using sampling depends heavily on the method chosen and the sampling rate applied. Striking the right balance between data fidelity and system efficiency is essential for any network that relies on flow sampling as part of its visibility and analytics strategy.

There are several main types of flow sampling techniques, each with distinct operational characteristics and implications for data accuracy. The most commonly used method is systematic sampling, where one out of every N packets is selected at fixed intervals. This deterministic approach is straightforward to implement and provides evenly spaced samples across the traffic stream. Because of its predictability, systematic sampling ensures that all periods of network activity receive attention, assuming traffic is consistent and evenly distributed. However, this very predictability can become a drawback in certain scenarios, as it may miss short-lived flows that do not align with the sampling window or fail to detect anomalies that occur between sampled packets.

Another widely used method is random sampling, where each packet has an equal probability of being selected, independent of its position in the traffic stream. This probabilistic technique avoids the regularity of systematic sampling and can offer better representation of bursty or irregular traffic. Random sampling tends to capture a more statistically unbiased view of the network, especially over large volumes of data. It is particularly useful in detecting transient events and understanding distributions that change rapidly. However, random sampling can result in clustering of samples or periods of low visibility, which may affect real-time analysis or short-duration flow identification.

Hash-based sampling offers another technique, often applied at the flow level rather than the packet level. In this method, a hash function is applied to packet header fields such as source and destination IP addresses or ports. The result is used to decide whether the flow should be sampled. This technique ensures that all packets belonging to a selected flow are consistently captured, preserving the flow's integrity while still reducing the overall number of flows being monitored. Hash-based sampling is particularly advantageous in applications where complete visibility into sampled flows is necessary for session-based analysis or security correlation. However, it may introduce bias if the hash function or selection criteria disproportionately include or exclude certain types of flows.

Stratified sampling is a more advanced method, involving the division of traffic into categories or strata based on criteria such as protocol type, source region, or traffic class. Sampling is then performed independently within each stratum to ensure proportional representation. This technique can enhance accuracy by ensuring that important or underrepresented traffic types are not overlooked. For instance, administrative or control traffic may be sampled at a higher rate than bulk data transfers. Stratified sampling introduces greater complexity into the sampling infrastructure but offers improved visibility for networks with diverse traffic patterns or critical service-level monitoring requirements.

The sampling rate, usually expressed as 1 out of N, plays a central role in determining the accuracy and utility of the sampled data. A lower sampling rate (e.g., 1 out of 10) captures more data and provides higher accuracy but places greater demand on system resources. A higher sampling rate (e.g., 1 out of 1,000 or 1 out of 10,000) reduces load but may result in significant gaps in visibility, particularly for low-volume or short-lived flows. The choice of sampling rate must consider the bandwidth of monitored links, the capabilities of exporting devices, the storage and processing power of collectors, and the goals of the analysis. In general, higher-speed links require more aggressive sampling to maintain performance, but this must be counterbalanced by the need for precise and actionable data.

Accuracy in flow sampling does not only refer to raw statistical precision. It also encompasses how well the sampled data represents real network behavior and supports operational objectives. For example, in a security context, missing even a single communication with a known malicious domain could lead to a missed detection. In a performance monitoring scenario, inaccuracies in latency or jitter measurements due to infrequent sampling may lead to poor user experience. Therefore, organizations must carefully evaluate how their sampling configurations align with their monitoring goals. Where critical flows must always be visible, exceptions may be made to sample them at a lower rate or to monitor them continuously.

To compensate for the reduced data fidelity inherent in sampling, most flow collectors and analytics tools apply extrapolation techniques. These involve multiplying observed values by the inverse of the sampling rate to estimate total traffic volumes or session counts. While this method works well for aggregate metrics, it may not restore the granularity required for fine-grained forensic analysis. Additionally, extrapolation assumes that sampled packets are a statistically valid representation of the whole, which may not hold true in all network environments, particularly those with skewed or unpredictable traffic patterns. Collectors may also use statistical smoothing, historical baselines, or anomaly detection algorithms to validate sampled data and filter out potential inaccuracies.

Some monitoring solutions combine multiple sampling techniques or dynamically adjust sampling rates based on network conditions. Adaptive sampling mechanisms increase visibility during abnormal traffic spikes or suspected events, allowing for deeper inspection when needed while maintaining efficiency during normal operations. This dynamic approach is particularly useful in environments where workloads and communication patterns are highly variable, such as cloud data centers, enterprise WANs, or virtualized networks. By responding to real-time telemetry, adaptive sampling can improve the balance between performance and visibility without requiring manual intervention.

Flow sampling remains a cornerstone of scalable network monitoring, enabling visibility across massive infrastructures without compromising performance. While sampling introduces trade-offs in accuracy, the choice of technique, sampling rate, and analytic approach can dramatically affect the quality and usefulness of the data. Designing effective flow sampling strategies requires a deep understanding of the network's architecture, traffic behaviors, operational priorities, and available tools. By aligning sampling practices with specific use cases, network administrators and security teams can ensure that their monitoring systems remain both efficient and insightful, even as traffic continues to grow in volume and complexity.

Configuring sFlow on Network Devices

Setting up sFlow on network devices is a crucial step in enabling scalable and efficient visibility across a network infrastructure. As a packet sampling protocol, sFlow offers real-time insight into network usage, application behavior, and potential anomalies without placing significant resource demands on the device. The configuration process, while conceptually straightforward, requires a clear understanding of both the hardware and the operational requirements of the monitoring system. Since sFlow operates through the collaboration between sFlow agents embedded in network devices and sFlow collectors that receive and analyze the sampled data, ensuring that both ends are configured correctly is essential for reliable monitoring.

The first stage in configuring sFlow involves determining which network devices support the protocol and identifying the interfaces that will be monitored. Many modern switches and routers from vendors such as HPE, Arista, Juniper, Brocade, and others offer native support for sFlow, typically through a command-line interface or web-based management system. It is important to verify that the firmware version installed on the device includes sFlow support, as some older versions may lack the necessary features. Once compatibility is confirmed, configuration begins with enabling the sFlow agent on the device and defining the collector's IP address and port. The collector is the destination to which all sFlow datagrams will be sent, and it must be reachable from the network device either directly or through proper routing.

The collector IP address is usually defined globally on the device, along with the UDP port number used for sFlow data export. The standard default port for sFlow is 6343, although some organizations may use alternate ports for organizational or security reasons. After setting the export destination, the next step is to define the sampling rate. This parameter determines how frequently packets are selected for analysis. For instance, a sampling rate of 1 out of 1000 means that, on average, one packet out of every thousand observed is sampled and exported. Choosing the correct sampling rate is critical. Lower sampling rates provide more granular visibility but increase the amount of exported data and processing load. Higher sampling rates reduce overhead but may miss short-lived flows or subtle anomalies.

Sampling rates can be applied globally or on a per-interface basis, depending on the platform. Applying different sampling rates to different interfaces is especially useful in heterogeneous environments. For example, backbone or uplink interfaces that carry large volumes of traffic may require higher sampling rates to avoid data saturation, while edge ports or server-facing interfaces can be monitored with greater granularity. Some devices allow administrators to set maximum and minimum thresholds to control the amount of sFlow data generated, ensuring the device continues to perform optimally under heavy load.

Beyond packet sampling, sFlow also includes counter polling, which involves collecting interface statistics such as byte and packet counts, errors, discards, and speed. These counters provide essential baseline data for bandwidth monitoring, trend analysis, and traffic engineering. The counter polling interval determines how frequently the agent collects and exports this data. Typical values range from 20 to 30 seconds, but this can be adjusted based on the organization's monitoring objectives. Frequent polling provides more up-to-date data but generates more export traffic, which must be managed carefully to prevent unnecessary overhead on the device and the network.

After defining the collector, sampling rate, and polling interval, the configuration must bind the sFlow settings to specific interfaces. On most platforms, this step involves entering the interface configuration mode and explicitly applying the sFlow agent. In some cases, enabling sFlow globally will automatically apply it to all interfaces, though this depends on the vendor and device model. Administrators should ensure that only relevant interfaces are included in the monitoring scope to reduce noise and focus analysis on the most critical parts of the network.

Some devices support multiple collectors, allowing the same sFlow data to be sent to more than one destination. This is useful for redundancy, parallel analysis, or integration with multiple monitoring tools. For example, one collector may feed a central analytics dashboard, while another forwards flow records to a security information and event management system. In such cases, careful planning is needed to ensure bandwidth and processing capacity are not exceeded, especially if multiple collectors are located across different segments of the network.

Once configuration is complete, testing and validation are essential. Administrators should verify that sFlow datagrams are being received by the collector and that the sampled data corresponds with expected traffic patterns. Packet capture tools or network telemetry software can be used to confirm that sFlow exports are reaching the collector and being interpreted correctly. Most network operating systems include commands to view the current sFlow configuration, display statistics about sampling and export activity, and check for errors or dropped packets. These tools assist in troubleshooting and fine-tuning the configuration.

It is also important to monitor the resource usage on the network device after enabling sFlow. Although sFlow is designed to be lightweight, exporting a large volume of sampled data over a long period can still impact device performance, particularly on older or lower-end hardware. Monitoring CPU and memory usage, as well as interface throughput, helps identify any adverse effects of the configuration. If necessary, sampling rates and polling intervals can be adjusted to optimize performance without sacrificing too much visibility.

Finally, documentation and change management should not be overlooked. All sFlow configurations should be documented clearly, including sampling rates, polling intervals, collector addresses, and monitored interfaces. This ensures that changes can be tracked over time and makes troubleshooting easier in case of issues. Centralized configuration management tools or automation platforms can help standardize sFlow deployment across multiple devices and enforce consistent monitoring policies.

Configuring sFlow on network devices is a foundational task in building a robust and scalable monitoring infrastructure. It empowers organizations to observe real-time traffic behavior, detect anomalies, and make informed decisions about performance and security. With proper configuration, validation, and ongoing maintenance, sFlow enables comprehensive visibility while preserving the efficiency and reliability of the network. As networks continue to grow in speed and complexity, sFlow remains a versatile and effective solution for organizations seeking to maintain control and clarity in their digital environments.

Analyzing sFlow Data for Network Insights

Analyzing sFlow data provides a powerful and scalable method for understanding real-time network behavior, identifying performance bottlenecks, detecting security threats, and supporting capacity planning across complex infrastructures. sFlow data is unique because it combines two primary types of information: sampled packet headers and interface counters. Together, these datasets allow administrators to obtain a representative view of traffic flows and interface-level metrics without the overhead associated with full packet capture or stateful flow tracking. Because sFlow data is continuously exported by enabled devices, it delivers ongoing visibility into network activity, making it well-suited for dynamic and high-speed environments such as data centers, enterprise WANs, and campus networks.

The process of analyzing sFlow data begins with its collection and normalization by a centralized sFlow collector. The collector receives sFlow datagrams from multiple agents distributed across the network, each containing randomly sampled packet headers and statistical counter information. The first analytical step is to decode these datagrams and extract key elements such as source and destination IP addresses, protocol types, source and destination ports, interface identifiers, MAC addresses, VLAN tags, and packet sizes. Since each packet sample represents a fraction of the overall traffic, these fields must be interpreted with awareness of the configured sampling rate to extrapolate meaningful metrics such as total byte counts, session volumes, or bandwidth usage.

Once normalized, the sampled data is aggregated to reveal patterns and trends. For example, administrators can group traffic by source IP to determine which hosts are generating the most traffic or by destination port to identify the most used applications and services. These aggregations can be visualized in dashboards that display top talkers, top protocols, bandwidth consumption per interface, or geographical traffic distribution. With consistent sampling across the environment, these visualizations can highlight shifts in traffic behavior over time, such as changes in usage due to application rollouts, remote work transitions, or infrastructure upgrades.

The interface counters included in sFlow data complement packet samples by offering baseline statistics on traffic volume, errors, discards, and interface utilization. These counters are polled at regular intervals and provide absolute values that help calibrate the estimated metrics derived from packet samples. Comparing counter data against sample-based estimates can validate the accuracy of extrapolated measurements and detect discrepancies that may point to sampling misconfigurations or anomalous behavior. For example, if the total packet count on an interface suddenly increases while the volume of sampled packets remains constant, it could indicate that the sampling rate needs adjustment or that a spike in traffic is occurring.

One of the most valuable aspects of sFlow analysis is the ability to detect anomalies in real time. Because sFlow provides a continuous stream of packet samples, analysis tools can establish baselines for typical traffic behavior and then identify deviations that suggest performance degradation or security incidents. For example, an unexpected increase in DNS query traffic from a single host could signal malware beaconing activity. A sudden burst of ICMP traffic might indicate scanning behavior. Likewise, a shift in application usage patterns, such as a sharp rise in file transfer traffic, might suggest unauthorized data movement. These indicators are often visible in sFlow data before they become noticeable through traditional SNMP-based monitoring systems.

Analyzing sFlow data is also essential for diagnosing performance issues. Packet samples reveal the distribution of traffic across different services and paths, helping administrators identify overloaded interfaces, asymmetric routing, or congestion points. sFlow provides insights into application-layer activity by capturing port numbers and protocol identifiers, enabling performance baselines for web services, email, voice over IP, and other enterprise applications. In the case of latency-sensitive services such as video conferencing or VoIP, sFlow can help detect jitter patterns, dropped packets, or traffic shaping policies that impact quality of experience. By correlating these findings with timestamps, interface identifiers, and protocol distributions, root causes can be isolated more quickly and resolved more effectively.

Capacity planning and trend analysis also benefit from sFlow-based monitoring. By continuously collecting and storing sampled data over time, organizations can track growth in bandwidth demand, shifts in application usage, and evolving traffic patterns. This long-term visibility supports decisions about infrastructure investment, such as upgrading WAN links, deploying new hardware, or moving workloads to the cloud. For example, identifying that a particular branch consistently operates at 85% link utilization during business hours may justify upgrading the connection or implementing quality of service policies. Similarly, observing a steady rise in encrypted traffic may inform security planning and the need for deeper inspection tools.

Another powerful dimension of sFlow analysis is its support for multi-tenant or segmented environments. By tagging sampled data with VLAN IDs or VRF identifiers, administrators can monitor traffic within and between isolated zones such as departments, customers, or virtual networks. This capability is crucial in environments like service provider networks or cloud data centers, where ensuring visibility into each tenant's traffic without violating privacy boundaries is mandatory. sFlow allows for traffic attribution at scale, supporting usage-based billing, SLA verification, and security auditing without capturing payload content.

Security analytics based on sFlow data continues to grow in relevance, particularly as organizations face increasingly sophisticated threats. sFlow's broad visibility allows for early detection of lateral movement, unauthorized access, data exfiltration attempts, and command-and-control communication. By integrating sFlow data with threat intelligence platforms and correlating it with indicators of compromise, security teams can identify hosts communicating with known malicious domains, using suspicious ports, or exhibiting abnormal traffic behavior. Because sFlow captures real-time activity from across the network, it provides context for security alerts and supports rapid incident response by identifying which systems are involved and how traffic has flowed through the environment.

Modern sFlow analysis platforms often incorporate machine learning and behavioral analytics to automate anomaly detection. These systems learn what constitutes normal network behavior and then alert administrators when statistically significant deviations occur. For example, if a user typically sends 100 MB of data per day but suddenly transfers several gigabytes, the system can flag this as a potential data leakage event. Such proactive analytics reduce the reliance on static thresholds or manual investigation and enable faster identification of issues that might otherwise go unnoticed.

Interpreting sFlow data accurately also requires understanding the limitations and implications of sampling. Sampling inherently introduces a degree of uncertainty, especially with small or short-lived flows. Analysts must account for the sampling rate in their calculations and recognize that rare events may go undetected unless sampling is configured appropriately. Therefore, part of effective sFlow analysis is tuning the sampling configuration to match the desired level of visibility while maintaining performance and scalability. Many platforms include built-in compensation algorithms that scale up observed values based on the sampling rate to estimate total traffic volumes more accurately.

Analyzing sFlow data opens a comprehensive window into the operational, security, and performance aspects of a network. Its efficiency and scalability make it well-suited for continuous monitoring across diverse network architectures. By leveraging sampled packet headers and interface counters, organizations gain the ability to make data-driven decisions, resolve issues swiftly, and adapt to changing demands. Whether used for operational diagnostics, long-term planning, or security forensics, sFlow analysis remains an essential practice for any network aiming to maintain visibility, performance, and resilience.

Advantages and Limitations of sFlow

sFlow is a powerful and efficient network monitoring technology that has become widely adopted due to its scalability, flexibility, and ability to provide real-time visibility into network traffic. It operates by using statistical sampling methods to capture packet headers and interface counters, offering a lightweight alternative to full-packet capture or stateful flow tracking protocols. Designed to handle high-throughput environments, sFlow has proven its value in data centers, campus networks, cloud infrastructures, and large enterprise environments. While sFlow brings significant benefits to network monitoring and analysis, it also comes with certain limitations that must be understood to ensure it is deployed effectively and used within appropriate contexts.

One of the primary advantages of sFlow is its minimal impact on network devices and infrastructure. Unlike protocols that maintain state for every network flow, sFlow samples packets at a configurable rate, significantly reducing the amount of processing and memory required on switches and routers. This makes it suitable for deployment in high-performance environments where devices are expected to forward traffic at line rate without interruption. The simplicity of its design allows sFlow to be implemented in hardware, enabling rapid and efficient sampling even on interfaces operating at speeds of 10 Gbps, 40 Gbps, or higher. The reduction in processing overhead also translates to cost savings, as it allows for more modest hardware to support extensive monitoring.

Another key benefit of sFlow is its scalability. By exporting a small percentage of traffic rather than all traffic flows, sFlow ensures that both the device and the collector can operate effectively without being overwhelmed by data. This makes it ideal for environments where thousands of ports or devices are generating traffic simultaneously. Whether monitoring an entire campus or a geographically distributed network, sFlow enables comprehensive visibility with a centralized collector receiving data from numerous distributed agents. The protocol's vendor-neutral nature, supported by the sFlow.org specification, enhances this scalability by allowing interoperability between equipment from different manufacturers. This is particularly advantageous in multi-vendor environments where standardization is necessary for centralized management and analysis.

Real-time monitoring is another core strength of sFlow. Because packet samples and interface counters are exported continuously and immediately, sFlow provides near real-time insights into network behavior. This allows administrators to respond quickly to issues such as congestion, misconfigurations, security threats, or anomalous activity. The ability to capture instantaneous snapshots of packet headers also makes sFlow effective for identifying protocols in use, detecting unexpected services, or diagnosing application-level performance problems. In dynamic and fast-moving network environments, the speed at which sFlow data is made available to collectors enhances the effectiveness of operational monitoring and incident response.

The richness of the data collected is also notable. sFlow does not limit itself to IP-layer visibility. It captures Layer 2 information such as MAC addresses, VLAN tags, and Ethernet types, making it useful in environments where Layer 2 traffic is significant. This holistic visibility is essential in modern networks where overlay technologies, virtualization, and microsegmentation are widely deployed. With appropriate analysis tools, sFlow data can be used for application performance monitoring, capacity planning, usage tracking, traffic engineering, and security auditing, all from the same stream of sampled data.

Despite these advantages, sFlow has limitations that must be considered when designing a monitoring strategy. The most significant limitation stems from its reliance on packet sampling. Because only a fraction of packets are captured, sFlow cannot provide complete flow records or full session reconstruction. This limitation makes it unsuitable for use cases that require precise flow-level details, such as certain security forensic investigations, application-layer troubleshooting, or regulatory compliance scenarios where full traceability is required. Small flows or those of short duration may not be sampled at all, leading to gaps in visibility. While statistical extrapolation can estimate overall traffic behavior, it cannot substitute for exact records in environments where deterministic data is necessary.

Another limitation involves the randomness of sampling. Even though probabilistic sampling is generally reliable over time, it can result in uneven data coverage in short-term analysis. Important events that occur between sampling intervals may go undetected, especially when high sampling rates are used. This poses challenges for detecting low-frequency threats, such as slow port scans or stealthy data exfiltration. It also limits the accuracy of per-user or per-application metrics in scenarios where precise measurements are essential. While adjusting the sampling rate can improve granularity, doing so increases the data volume and processing load, potentially impacting device performance and collector capacity.

The accuracy of data derived from sFlow also depends heavily on correct sampling rate configuration and consistent application across the network. If sampling rates differ significantly between devices or interfaces, the data collected may become difficult to normalize, leading to misleading results in aggregate reports or trend analyses. Furthermore, not all analysis tools are equally equipped to handle sampled data correctly. Some may fail to account for the sampling rate when calculating statistics, resulting in underreported or misrepresented traffic volumes. This emphasizes the importance of using monitoring platforms that are explicitly designed to work with sFlow and capable of interpreting the data accurately.

sFlow's reliance on external collectors and analysis tools is another consideration. The protocol itself does not define how data is stored, queried, or visualized. This means that the quality and depth of insights available from sFlow depend significantly on the capabilities of the monitoring solution in use. A weak or poorly configured collector may fail to scale with the volume of data received or may lack features to fully leverage the data captured. Organizations must ensure that their sFlow infrastructure includes not only properly configured agents but also robust, scalable, and intelligent collectors that can provide actionable insights in a timely manner.

In some contexts, the lack of payload data in sFlow samples is also a limitation. While this omission improves privacy and reduces storage and processing demands, it also restricts the protocol's usefulness for deep packet inspection, application-layer forensics, or content-based threat detection. For environments where the ability to inspect full payloads is necessary—such as intrusion detection, data loss prevention, or content filtering—sFlow must be supplemented with other tools that can perform these functions. This complementary approach is common in security architectures that balance performance with visibility.

Overall, sFlow delivers a valuable combination of speed, scalability, and efficiency for modern network monitoring. Its strengths lie in its ability to deliver broad, real-time visibility with low overhead, making it suitable for large-scale deployments and continuous monitoring. However, its sampling-based design and limited support for detailed flow records or payload analysis mean it is not a one-size-fits-all solution. Organizations that adopt sFlow must understand its capabilities and constraints, aligning its use with operational objectives and integrating it with complementary tools to build a complete and effective monitoring strategy. By doing so, they can fully leverage sFlow's advantages while mitigating its limitations.

Practical Applications of sFlow in Large Networks

In large-scale networks, managing performance, ensuring security, and maintaining visibility over traffic flows becomes increasingly complex. As organizations expand their infrastructure to accommodate more users, devices, and applications, the need for efficient, scalable, and real-time monitoring grows exponentially. sFlow, with its ability to sample packets and gather interface counters with minimal overhead, proves to be an effective solution for these environments. Its low impact on network devices and broad support across vendor platforms make it an ideal protocol for monitoring diverse and high-speed environments, including data centers, enterprise WANs, university campuses, service provider backbones, and cloud infrastructures. The practical applications of sFlow in such networks are vast, enabling operations teams to address performance, capacity, security, and compliance challenges in ways that are both proactive and responsive.

One of the most significant applications of sFlow in large networks is real-time traffic visibility. Because sFlow continuously exports packet samples and counter data, it provides immediate insights into which applications are using the network, how much bandwidth is being consumed, and which hosts are generating or receiving traffic. This visibility allows network administrators to identify top talkers, monitor application usage trends, and assess traffic patterns across different segments of the network. In a campus network with thousands of users, for instance, sFlow can help determine whether video streaming, file transfers, or peer-to-peer applications are consuming bandwidth that would otherwise be allocated to academic or business-critical services. This level of awareness supports informed decision-making around traffic shaping policies, firewall rules, or quality of service configurations.

Another critical use of sFlow is in performance monitoring and troubleshooting. When users report slow application response times or inconsistent connectivity, sFlow provides a detailed picture of where traffic is flowing and how it is behaving. By analyzing sampled packets and interface counters, engineers can quickly determine if there is congestion on a specific link, if routing is asymmetric, or if an application is behaving abnormally. For example, in a large data center with multiple redundant paths, sFlow can reveal imbalances in load distribution that affect certain virtual machines or tenants. It can also show when certain interfaces experience microbursts or transient traffic spikes that are invisible to SNMP or polling-based tools. This granular and time-sensitive visibility allows for faster root cause analysis and resolution, reducing mean time to repair and minimizing user impact.

Capacity planning and bandwidth forecasting are also enhanced through sFlow. By collecting continuous data over time, organizations can build comprehensive historical records of traffic usage. These records support the identification of growth trends, peak usage periods, and emerging bandwidth demands. In large networks where link saturation can degrade service levels, understanding long-term utilization patterns helps justify infrastructure investments or the reallocation of resources. For instance, if sFlow reveals that a specific WAN link consistently operates at over 80 percent utilization during business hours, it may prompt an upgrade to a higher-capacity circuit or the deployment of WAN optimization techniques. Similarly, if certain services or departments consume significantly more bandwidth than anticipated, IT leadership can assess whether those needs align with business objectives or require policy enforcement.

In multi-tenant environments such as service providers or cloud hosting platforms, sFlow enables detailed traffic attribution and usage accounting. Each customer or tenant may have isolated network segments, virtual machines, or containerized workloads, all of which contribute to overall traffic. sFlow can be used to monitor these isolated zones individually, using VLAN IDs, VRFs, or IP address ranges to differentiate tenants. This capability allows providers to enforce service level agreements, generate usage-based billing reports, and detect violations of acceptable use policies. When combined with automation and orchestration tools, sFlow also facilitates real-time feedback loops that dynamically adjust network policies or resource allocations based on actual usage, improving efficiency and customer experience.

Security monitoring is another area where sFlow proves invaluable in large networks. The protocol's ability to provide a broad, continuous, and distributed view of network activity makes it ideal for detecting anomalies, identifying threats, and supporting forensic investigations. In a network with thousands of endpoints, traditional security tools may struggle to detect subtle indicators of compromise. sFlow can reveal patterns such as a sudden increase in outbound traffic from a single host, unusual port usage, communication with known malicious IPs, or scanning activity. Because packet headers are captured in real time, even short-lived connections that might evade log-based detection can be observed and analyzed. When integrated with threat intelligence platforms or SIEM systems, sFlow enables early detection of attacks and rapid response actions

sFlow also plays a vital role in validating network segmentation and policy enforcement. In large enterprises or data centers with complex segmentation strategies, ensuring that traffic remains within designated boundaries is critical for both performance and security. sFlow data can verify whether access control lists, firewall rules, or VLAN policies are functioning as intended. If traffic is observed between zones that should be isolated, it may indicate a misconfiguration or breach. This validation is especially important in regulated industries where segmentation is mandated for compliance, such as in healthcare, finance, or government networks. By continuously monitoring flow paths, sFlow provides assurance that segmentation strategies are being enforced correctly.

Application performance management is yet another area where sFlow offers practical benefits. As enterprises increasingly rely on distributed and cloud-native applications, visibility into how traffic moves between microservices, across data centers, or into external SaaS platforms becomes critical. sFlow provides insights into latency, packet loss, and jitter, particularly for applications that use known ports or protocols. This allows network and application teams to collaborate more effectively, using shared data to diagnose issues that might span both network and application domains. When deployed alongside performance baselines and synthetic monitoring tools, sFlow enhances end-to-end visibility and ensures that user experience is maintained even as infrastructure evolves.

Another practical application is in automating network operations. With continuous data streams from sFlow agents feeding into analytics platforms and automation engines, organizations can build intelligent systems that respond to changing conditions without human intervention. For instance, if sFlow detects a link becoming saturated, the system could trigger a policy to reroute traffic, spin up additional virtual network functions, or notify administrators of the change. This automation enhances agility, reduces human error, and supports the operational demands of hybrid cloud, SD-WAN, and intent-based networking strategies.

In very large networks, where visibility gaps can have significant operational or financial consequences, sFlow provides a highly effective and low-impact method to maintain awareness of how the network is behaving. Its practical applications span real-time monitoring, long-term planning, security enforcement, and performance assurance. When properly implemented and supported by capable analytics tools, sFlow becomes not just a telemetry mechanism, but a foundation for intelligent, adaptive, and resilient network operations. It allows teams to shift from reactive troubleshooting to proactive management, providing the insight necessary to support both current demands and future growth.

Introduction to Network Telemetry

Network telemetry has emerged as a transformative concept in the realm of network monitoring and management. As networks have grown in scale, complexity, and performance demands, traditional approaches to visibility such as SNMP polling, syslog collection, and manual inspection have proven inadequate for providing the depth, precision, and speed necessary for proactive operations. Network telemetry represents a fundamental shift from reactive, pull-based monitoring methods to proactive, push-based, high-frequency data collection mechanisms. It provides continuous streams of rich, structured data directly from devices to collectors or analysis platforms, offering unparalleled insight into the health, behavior, and performance of the network infrastructure.

The essence of network telemetry lies in its ability to gather and export detailed operational data in real time. Instead of relying on periodic queries or waiting for alerts after an issue has already impacted users, telemetry-capable devices stream relevant data to external systems, enabling immediate visibility into anomalies, configuration changes, traffic fluctuations, and system faults. This shift toward streaming, time-series data transforms how network teams detect, diagnose, and respond to problems. Telemetry facilitates earlier detection of issues and supports faster root cause analysis, minimizing the mean time to repair and enhancing the overall user experience.

One of the key features of network telemetry is its granularity. Traditional monitoring tools are often limited in what they can collect, constrained by polling intervals, device limitations, or fixed data models. Telemetry, in contrast, allows for customizable data exports. Operators can define exactly which metrics to collect, from which components, and at what frequency. This enables deep visibility into everything from interface counters and queue depths to CPU usage, temperature sensors, and error states. The ability to tailor the telemetry feed ensures that organizations capture precisely the data they need without overwhelming the collection infrastructure with irrelevant information. This customization also reduces blind spots, as operators are no longer confined to the static datasets provided by legacy protocols.

Performance and scalability are critical drivers behind the adoption of network telemetry. As traffic volumes surge and networks span multiple geographic regions and hybrid cloud environments, the need for scalable and efficient visibility grows. Traditional polling models, which query devices every few minutes, cannot scale to hundreds or thousands of interfaces without introducing lag or causing performance overhead. In contrast, telemetry leverages lightweight, event-driven mechanisms that can stream thousands of data points per second with minimal impact on device resources. This allows operators to monitor far more elements of the network, across more locations, at much higher frequency, all without degrading the performance of the devices themselves.

Another important dimension of network telemetry is its integration with advanced analytics platforms. The raw data generated by telemetry streams can be ingested into time-series databases, big data platforms, machine learning engines, or visualization tools. This integration enables real-time dashboards, automated anomaly detection, and predictive analytics. By continuously analyzing trends and detecting patterns in telemetry data, network teams can anticipate issues before they affect users, plan capacity expansions more effectively, and uncover root causes that would otherwise remain hidden. The continuous nature of telemetry feeds also ensures that data gaps are minimized, improving the fidelity of any analytical outputs and reducing the likelihood of false positives or missed events.

Telemetry also plays a pivotal role in modern automation and orchestration frameworks. As networks evolve toward software-defined, intent-based, and self-healing models, real-time feedback becomes essential. Telemetry provides the observability backbone that allows these systems to verify the state of the network, validate policy enforcement, and make informed decisions about configuration changes or traffic rerouting. For example, if telemetry reveals that a particular link is experiencing congestion or packet loss, the automation controller can dynamically shift traffic to an alternate path without waiting for a manual response. Similarly, if device health metrics indicate a hardware failure is imminent, the system can trigger preemptive maintenance workflows. This tight coupling between observability and control is a hallmark of next-generation network architectures.

Vendor support for telemetry has grown rapidly in recent years, with major network equipment manufacturers integrating telemetry capabilities into their hardware and software platforms. Cisco, Juniper, Arista, Nokia, and others offer support for protocols such as gRPC, gNMI, and OpenConfig, which standardize the way telemetry data is collected and consumed. These standards promote interoperability, allowing telemetry data from multiple vendors to be aggregated and analyzed using unified tools. In addition to structured device-level telemetry, some vendors provide flow-level telemetry, enabling deep insights into traffic behaviors, application performance, and user interactions. This convergence of device and flow telemetry provides a more comprehensive view of network activity and performance.

Security monitoring is another area that benefits significantly from network telemetry. Because telemetry provides high-fidelity, real-time data, it enables early detection of security threats that might evade traditional log-based monitoring. For example, unusual spikes in CPU usage, unexpected configuration changes, or anomalies in interface statistics can all signal the early stages of a breach or compromise. When combined with machine learning and behavioral analysis, telemetry data can uncover subtle indicators of advanced persistent threats, botnet activity, or data exfiltration. Furthermore, since telemetry data is structured and often timestamped with high precision, it supports accurate forensic investigations and rapid response actions, making it an essential component of any modern security operations center.

Another advantage of network telemetry is its suitability for cloud-native and hybrid environments. As workloads migrate to public and private clouds, maintaining consistent observability becomes a challenge. Telemetry solutions that support containerized applications, virtualized network functions, and API-driven infrastructures can extend visibility beyond traditional physical devices. This ensures that operators retain a complete picture of the network, regardless of where applications and users are located. In distributed environments where latency, jitter, and performance variation are common, telemetry provides the continuous feedback necessary to maintain service levels and enforce policy compliance across diverse infrastructure domains.

Despite its many benefits, implementing network telemetry does require planning and investment. Organizations must ensure they have the appropriate infrastructure to collect, store, and analyze telemetry data. This includes selecting collectors that can handle high-throughput data ingestion, databases that can efficiently store time-series metrics, and analytics tools that can turn raw data into actionable insights. Network teams also need to define clear objectives for their telemetry strategy, determining which metrics matter most and how the data will be used. With proper planning, telemetry not only enhances visibility but also strengthens the alignment between IT operations, business objectives, and user experience.

Network telemetry is fundamentally reshaping how networks are monitored and managed. By providing continuous, structured, and customizable data streams, it delivers the real-time insight necessary to maintain performance, ensure reliability, and support automation at scale. As digital infrastructure continues to grow in complexity, telemetry offers a scalable and future-proof approach to observability, empowering organizations to operate with confidence in a world of constant change.

Streaming Telemetry vs Polling-Based Models

The evolution of network monitoring tools and methodologies has been shaped by the need to balance visibility, scalability, and performance. For decades, polling-based models such as SNMP have been the default method for monitoring devices across enterprise networks. These models involve periodic requests sent by a central monitoring system to network devices, querying specific variables such as interface utilization, memory usage, or CPU load. While polling has served networks adequately in the past, the increasing speed, complexity, and dynamism of modern infrastructure have exposed its limitations. This has paved the way for streaming telemetry, a newer, more efficient method of collecting real-time data from network elements. Streaming telemetry fundamentally changes the model by allowing devices to push data to collectors in a continuous and structured format, eliminating the need for repeated polling requests and enabling a much richer and timelier view of network behavior.

Polling-based models rely on a request-response mechanism where the network monitoring system initiates communication and asks for data at defined intervals, often ranging from one minute to five minutes. This periodic nature creates gaps in visibility, during which transient events or performance anomalies can occur and disappear without being captured. Moreover, polling can create significant load on both the devices being queried and the network itself, particularly when large volumes of data are needed from many devices at once. Since polling frequency is often limited to avoid overloading the network and the devices, administrators are forced to make trade-offs between data granularity and system performance. For example, polling CPU usage every five minutes may be sufficient to detect long-term trends, but it may completely miss a short-lived spike that causes temporary performance degradation or application slowdown.

Streaming telemetry addresses these limitations by flipping the model. Instead of waiting for external queries, the device proactively sends data to a telemetry collector at predefined intervals or when specific conditions are met. This push-based model results in lower latency and higher granularity, as updates can be streamed as frequently as every few seconds or even milliseconds. More importantly, the data is structured, often using protocols like gNMI or gRPC, which allow for hierarchical, vendor-neutral representations of the device state. This structure not only simplifies data parsing but also supports extensibility, enabling operators to collect complex or custom data sets that were previously inaccessible via SNMP.

One of the core benefits of streaming telemetry is its ability to scale across large networks. Because it is event-driven and asynchronous, streaming does not require the monitoring system to initiate thousands of queries across the network. This dramatically reduces the overhead on both the collectors and the devices. Network devices are configured to send updates only when values change or at intervals that make sense for the metric being monitored. This efficient use of bandwidth and CPU cycles makes streaming telemetry ideal for environments with high interface counts, geographically distributed infrastructure, or performance-sensitive applications. Additionally, streaming telemetry supports subscription models, where operators define exactly which data they need and how often it should be sent. This selective approach reduces data volume and focuses resources on the most critical metrics.

Another area where streaming telemetry surpasses polling is in the timeliness and continuity of the data it delivers. Since updates are sent as soon as they are available, streaming telemetry can capture transient events that might last only a few seconds. In contrast, polling would have to operate at unreasonably high frequencies to achieve the same resolution, which would lead to excessive network and CPU load. The real-time nature of telemetry enables immediate awareness of anomalies, which is particularly valuable for modern operations centers focused on proactive problem detection and fast incident response. For example, telemetry can instantly reveal sudden changes in traffic volume, link flaps, or changes in routing table entries, allowing administrators to correlate issues faster and take action before user experience is affected.

Streaming telemetry also enables more advanced analytics and automation. Because the data is time-stamped and delivered in near-real-time, it integrates seamlessly with time-series databases, machine learning platforms, and AI-driven monitoring tools. This compatibility opens the door to predictive maintenance, capacity forecasting, and anomaly detection based on behavioral baselines. With polling, such capabilities are limited due to the coarse granularity and the uneven arrival times of data. Streaming data flows support continuous learning models that can detect subtle shifts in network behavior and flag potential issues before they escalate. Furthermore, telemetry feeds provide a foundational data layer for intent-based networking and closed-loop automation, where real-time state information is used to verify that network configurations match the intended policy and to trigger corrective actions automatically when deviations occur.

Despite its advantages, streaming telemetry is not without its challenges. Implementing telemetry requires modern hardware and software support on both the device and collector sides. Many legacy devices may not support streaming protocols, necessitating hardware upgrades or hybrid approaches where both telemetry and polling coexist. Additionally, the volume of data generated by frequent telemetry updates can be substantial, requiring robust infrastructure for collection, storage, and processing. Organizations must invest in scalable databases, message brokers, and analytic engines capable of ingesting and analyzing telemetry data in real time. There is also a learning curve associated with telemetry configuration, especially for teams accustomed to the simplicity of SNMP polling. However, the long-term benefits in visibility, responsiveness, and automation potential often justify the investment.

Security and data integrity are additional considerations in both models. Polling-based systems, particularly those using older versions of SNMP, are known to have weak authentication and encryption capabilities, making them vulnerable to spoofing or interception. Streaming telemetry, built on more modern protocols, often includes support for secure transport methods such as TLS, mutual authentication, and role-based access control. This enhances the confidentiality and integrity of the data being transmitted, aligning with the security requirements of modern enterprises. However, the centralized nature of telemetry collection also makes the collectors critical components that must be secured and protected against failure or compromise.

In comparing streaming telemetry and polling-based models, it becomes clear that streaming telemetry offers a more robust, scalable, and future-proof approach to network monitoring. It delivers higher-frequency, structured data with lower overhead and improved real-time visibility. While polling remains useful for certain legacy systems and simple metrics, its limitations in speed, scalability, and granularity make it less suitable for modern, high-performance networks. As organizations continue to adopt software-defined infrastructure, hybrid cloud, and automation-driven operations, streaming telemetry provides the observability foundation required to manage complexity, ensure performance, and maintain control in a fast-changing digital landscape.

Protocols Used in Telemetry Solutions

In the landscape of modern network monitoring, telemetry has become a cornerstone technology that allows for real-time, high-resolution visibility into the operational status of infrastructure. The effectiveness of telemetry depends heavily on the communication protocols used to collect, transport, and interpret data. These protocols define how telemetry information is structured, how it is transmitted from network devices to collectors, and how efficiently and securely it can be processed at scale. Unlike legacy protocols such as SNMP or syslog, which rely on periodic polling or unstructured logging, telemetry-specific protocols are designed to handle continuous data streams, hierarchical data models, and dynamic subscription-based reporting. As organizations move toward streaming telemetry architectures, the choice of protocol becomes critical in achieving the performance, flexibility, and interoperability required in diverse and complex environments.

Among the most prominent protocols used in telemetry solutions is gNMI, or gRPC Network Management Interface. Developed by the OpenConfig working group, gNMI is based on the gRPC transport framework and is designed to offer a standardized method for network devices to communicate structured state data to monitoring systems. gNMI leverages protocol buffers, which are a compact and efficient data serialization format, to encode telemetry messages. This results in reduced bandwidth consumption and improved processing speeds compared to text-based protocols. gNMI supports multiple operational models, including get, set, subscribe, and capabilities requests. The subscribe model is particularly relevant for telemetry, as it allows collectors to subscribe to specific data paths within the device and receive updates in real time. This reduces the need for repetitive polling and allows for near-instantaneous awareness of changes in network state.

Another widely used protocol in telemetry solutions is NETCONF, or Network Configuration Protocol. NETCONF is an IETF standard that facilitates the management of network devices using XML-based data models. While originally intended for configuration tasks, NETCONF can also be used for state retrieval, and when combined with YANG data models, it provides a powerful framework for both configuration and telemetry. NETCONF operates over a secure transport layer, typically SSH, ensuring the confidentiality and integrity of data exchanged between devices and management systems. Although not as lightweight as gNMI due to its reliance on XML, NETCONF remains popular in environments where existing systems are already integrated with it or where fine-grained configuration and telemetry control are required. Its transactional nature also enables safe and atomic operations, which are valuable in change-controlled environments.

Streaming telemetry solutions also often use the gRPC protocol independently of gNMI. gRPC is an open-source, high-performance RPC framework developed by Google that enables efficient communication between distributed systems. In telemetry, gRPC provides a reliable and low-latency transport mechanism for sending telemetry data from devices to collectors. Because it supports bidirectional streaming and multiplexing over a single connection, gRPC is ideal for environments with large numbers of telemetry subscriptions and high-frequency updates. It also supports strong encryption and authentication through TLS and mutual TLS, enhancing security for sensitive telemetry data. gRPC's compatibility with multiple programming languages and platforms makes it a versatile choice for both device vendors and telemetry application developers.

In addition to gNMI and NETCONF, many vendors and telemetry frameworks use protocols such as RESTCONF, which is a RESTful interface for accessing YANG-modeled data over HTTP. RESTCONF is easier to implement in web-based environments and supports CRUD operations through standard HTTP methods. While not typically used for high-frequency telemetry streaming due to the overhead of HTTP and JSON encoding, RESTCONF is useful for on-demand retrieval of network state or for interacting with devices in environments where lightweight REST APIs are preferred. It bridges the gap between traditional SNMP-based monitoring and modern structured data access, offering a path for gradual migration toward telemetry-driven observability.

Some legacy protocols have also been adapted or extended to support telemetry-like behavior. For example, SNMP itself has seen enhancements that attempt to offer notification-based or trap-driven data delivery. However, these extensions often fall short of the efficiency and scalability provided by true streaming telemetry protocols. Similarly, syslog, while still widely used for unstructured logging, is increasingly being supplemented by telemetry solutions that provide structured and filterable data with minimal latency. In practice, many organizations run these legacy protocols in parallel with newer telemetry mechanisms, using them for backward compatibility or as part of multi-layered observability strategies.

Message brokers and data transport protocols also play a key role in telemetry architecture. Protocols like Kafka, MQTT, and AMQP are frequently used in telemetry pipelines to decouple data producers from consumers, enable buffering and load distribution, and facilitate integration with analytics platforms. Kafka, in particular, has become a common backbone for telemetry data in large-scale environments due to its high throughput, durability, and scalability. Devices or agents stream telemetry data to Kafka topics, from which various consumers—ranging from visualization dashboards to machine learning engines—can subscribe and process the data in real time or batch modes. MQTT, known for its lightweight footprint, is often used in IoT telemetry scenarios where resource constraints and unreliable network conditions require minimal overhead.

Another critical component in telemetry protocols is the use of data modeling languages. YANG is the dominant modeling language used in most modern telemetry implementations. It allows for the creation of hierarchical, vendor-neutral schemas that define the structure and semantics of telemetry data. By using YANG models, network devices and management systems can agree on the data elements being collected, their types, and their relationships. This promotes interoperability and simplifies integration across multi-vendor environments. Devices that support OpenConfig YANG models can expose standardized telemetry paths, enabling consistent data collection regardless of hardware manufacturer.

Security considerations are central to the choice and implementation of telemetry protocols. Most modern protocols support encryption in transit, authentication, and authorization mechanisms to ensure that telemetry data is protected from tampering or interception. This is especially important in environments where telemetry data may include sensitive operational details, such as traffic patterns, configuration changes, or device health metrics. By adopting secure protocols and enforcing best practices for key management and access control, organizations can safeguard their telemetry infrastructure and ensure that the data remains trustworthy and confidential.

The choice of telemetry protocol has lasting implications for an organization's monitoring capabilities, operational efficiency, and future readiness. As networks become more dynamic, programmable, and distributed, telemetry protocols must support not only efficient data transport but also rich semantics, flexibility, and extensibility. Protocols like gNMI and gRPC represent the next generation of telemetry communication, enabling granular and real-time visibility at scale. When combined with robust data models, message transport frameworks, and analytics platforms, they form the foundation of modern observability architectures that drive automation, reliability, and strategic decision-making in complex network environments.

gRPC and Protocol Buffers in Telemetry

In the evolving field of network telemetry, achieving efficient, scalable, and real-time communication between devices and monitoring systems is essential. Traditional protocols that were built around polling and text-based message formats are no longer sufficient to meet the demands of modern, high-speed, distributed infrastructures. As telemetry solutions become more dynamic and data rich, there is a growing need for transport mechanisms and serialization methods that can support high-frequency data streams, low latency, and structured message formats. Two technologies that have rapidly gained prominence in this space are gRPC and Protocol Buffers. Together, they offer a powerful foundation for building robust telemetry architectures that are not only performant but also interoperable and extensible across diverse network environments.

gRPC, or Google Remote Procedure Call, is an open-source framework developed by Google to support efficient communication between distributed systems. At its core, gRPC allows clients and servers to interact using remote procedure calls, where a client can invoke functions or services on a remote server as if they were local. In the context of telemetry, gRPC serves as the transport mechanism that facilitates the exchange of telemetry data between devices such as routers, switches, and firewalls, and external telemetry collectors or analytics platforms. Unlike traditional HTTP-based communication, gRPC operates over HTTP/2, which supports features such as multiplexed streams, header compression, and bidirectional communication. These enhancements reduce overhead, improve latency, and allow for a more continuous and responsive data flow, all of which are critical in high-performance telemetry environments.

Protocol Buffers, or protobufs, are the serialization format typically used in conjunction with gRPC. Also developed by Google, Protocol Buffers define a compact and efficient binary format for encoding structured data. Compared to human-readable formats like JSON or XML, protobufs are significantly smaller and faster to serialize and deserialize. This efficiency translates to lower bandwidth usage and faster processing on both ends of the communication channel. In a telemetry scenario, where devices might be sending thousands of updates per second across hundreds of metrics, the performance advantage of Protocol Buffers is not just desirable but necessary. With protobufs, devices can stream structured telemetry data to collectors with minimal CPU and memory overhead, even in high-throughput conditions.

The synergy between gRPC and Protocol Buffers is evident in the way they facilitate real-time, bidirectional communication in telemetry workflows. A typical telemetry session begins with a client, such as a collector, subscribing to specific telemetry data points on a network device. These subscriptions are defined using gRPC calls, which are then maintained as persistent sessions over HTTP/2. As changes occur or as data is updated at the device level, the telemetry agent pushes updates to the collector in the form of serialized Protocol Buffer messages. These messages follow a schema that both ends understand, ensuring consistency and eliminating the need for manual parsing or custom data interpretation. The structured nature of the data also enables powerful filtering, aggregation, and transformation functions on the collector side, supporting more intelligent and automated analytics.

Another key advantage of using gRPC and Protocol Buffers in telemetry is their strong support for data modeling and extensibility. Protocol Buffers use .proto files to define the structure of the data being transmitted. These files act as contracts between devices and collectors, specifying the fields, data types, and hierarchical relationships within telemetry messages. This formalization simplifies integration and reduces errors, especially in multi-vendor or multi-domain environments. When telemetry requirements evolve or new data points are introduced, .proto files can be updated to include additional fields without breaking backward compatibility. This allows telemetry systems to grow and adapt over time without requiring major reconfiguration or redevelopment.

Security is another area where gRPC demonstrates its strengths. Built on HTTP/2, gRPC supports TLS encryption by default, ensuring that telemetry data remains secure in transit. Mutual TLS can also be configured to enforce client and server authentication, adding another layer of security. In telemetry deployments where data may include sensitive operational details, such as traffic patterns, device health, or user behavior, securing the communication channel is essential. The use of modern encryption and authentication standards ensures that telemetry data is not only accurate and timely but also protected against interception or tampering.

From a development and integration standpoint, gRPC and Protocol Buffers offer cross-platform compatibility and multi-language support. The protobuf compiler can generate client and server code in numerous programming languages, including Python, Go, Java, C++, and many others. This flexibility allows telemetry systems to be integrated into a wide variety of environments, from embedded systems on network devices to cloud-native applications and big data platforms. Whether the telemetry collector is part of a data center management system, a real-time analytics engine, or a machine learning pipeline, the consistency and performance of gRPC and Protocol Buffers enable seamless integration and data flow.

In large-scale telemetry architectures, the efficiency of gRPC and Protocol Buffers becomes even more critical. As organizations monitor hundreds or thousands of devices, the volume of telemetry data can reach millions of updates per minute. Legacy protocols struggle under this load, introducing latency, increasing error rates, and often missing critical events. gRPC's efficient transport and protobuf's compact serialization allow telemetry pipelines to handle these volumes with ease, maintaining high fidelity and low latency even under stress. This capability is especially important for use cases such as network anomaly detection, predictive maintenance, and automated policy enforcement, where decisions must be made in near real time.

Furthermore, gRPC enables advanced communication patterns that are valuable in telemetry. Its support for server-side streaming allows devices to continuously send data without repeated requests, which is ideal for continuous monitoring. Its client-side streaming and bidirectional streaming features also enable more complex interactions, such as negotiation of telemetry capabilities, dynamic subscription adjustments, or on-the-fly configuration changes. These patterns support adaptive and intelligent telemetry systems that can respond to changing network conditions, user demands, or security threats with agility and precision.

Overall, gRPC and Protocol Buffers represent a paradigm shift in how telemetry data is communicated and processed. They offer a combination of performance, structure, security, and extensibility that is unmatched by older protocols. In the context of modern network monitoring, where speed, accuracy, and scalability are essential, these technologies provide the foundation for telemetry systems that are not only responsive and efficient but also future-ready. As networks become more automated, virtualized, and distributed, the role of real-time telemetry will continue to expand, and gRPC with Protocol Buffers will remain central to enabling the next generation of observability and control.

YANG Data Models in Network Telemetry

YANG data models have become a foundational element in the evolution of network telemetry, playing a pivotal role in how modern network infrastructure is monitored, configured, and managed. As networks have grown more complex and dynamic, the need for structured, machine-readable representations of device configuration and operational state has become increasingly clear. Traditional methods of device management relied heavily on vendor-specific implementations, static MIBs, or loosely structured log messages, all of which limited interoperability and consistency. YANG, which stands for Yet Another Next Generation, is a data modeling language developed by the IETF to standardize the way configuration and state data is described across different types of network devices. It allows for the precise and hierarchical definition of data, making it ideally suited for telemetry applications that require granular, real-time observability across a multi-vendor environment.

One of the core strengths of YANG is its ability to express complex data structures in a clear and extensible way. It supports the definition of containers, lists, leaf nodes, and groupings, which together allow the model to reflect the actual organization of network configuration and state information within a device. YANG models can describe not only individual parameters such as interface speeds or CPU usage, but also their relationships, constraints, and contextual meaning. This rich expressiveness is essential in telemetry, where accuracy and structure are paramount. When used in conjunction with protocols like NETCONF, RESTCONF, or gNMI, YANG models serve as the blueprint for what data is available from the device, how it is organized, and how it can be queried or streamed to a collector.

In network telemetry, YANG provides the foundation for defining what telemetry data is exposed by a device and how it is encoded and transmitted. Each YANG model specifies a schema that can be mapped to a tree-like structure of data paths. These paths correspond to real-time metrics such as interface counters, memory usage, routing tables, or queue depths. Through subscriptions to these paths, telemetry collectors can receive continuous updates about the operational state of the device. Because the YANG model defines the format and semantics of the data, both the sender and receiver have a shared understanding of what the data represents, reducing ambiguity and simplifying integration with analytics platforms.

Another advantage of using YANG in telemetry is its support for modularity and reusability. YANG modules can be developed independently and then imported or augmented to create more comprehensive models. This approach allows vendors, standards bodies, and network operators to collaboratively develop data models that are both standardized and adaptable to specific needs. The OpenConfig initiative, for instance, has developed a set of vendor-neutral YANG models that describe common network elements such as interfaces, BGP, QoS, and system health. These models are widely supported and form the basis for many telemetry implementations. By using OpenConfig models, operators can ensure consistency in their telemetry data regardless of the underlying vendor, reducing the operational complexity of managing heterogeneous environments.

Validation and constraint checking are also enhanced through YANG. The language allows for the inclusion of type restrictions, mandatory fields, default values, and range limits. These constraints ensure that the telemetry data adheres to expected formats and values, improving data quality and reliability. In real-world telemetry deployments, where high volumes of data are transmitted continuously, having structured validation mechanisms helps to filter out anomalies, catch misconfigurations early, and maintain the integrity of the monitoring system. This is particularly important when telemetry data is fed into automated decision-making systems or machine learning engines, where bad data can lead to inaccurate predictions or unintended actions.

The adoption of YANG data models has significantly improved the automation capabilities of telemetry systems. Because YANG provides a programmatic interface to device capabilities and state, it can be used to dynamically generate subscriptions, adapt data collection strategies, and integrate with orchestration platforms. For example, a network controller can use YANG-defined paths to subscribe to changes in device health or link utilization and trigger remediation actions in real time. This tight integration between telemetry, automation, and control systems is essential for implementing closed-loop automation and intent-based networking. In such environments, YANG acts as the common language that enables consistent communication and coordination across all layers of the network stack.

Security and access control are also enhanced through YANG's structured approach. By defining access control models and read/write permissions within the YANG schema, network administrators can enforce fine-grained access to telemetry data. This means that sensitive data can be protected while still allowing open access to less critical information, depending on the user role or application context. Combined with secure transport protocols like SSH for NETCONF or TLS for gNMI, YANG-based telemetry systems can meet the rigorous security requirements of enterprise and service provider networks.

In terms of implementation, YANG data models are compiled into schema trees that are used by network devices to expose their capabilities to external systems. Tools such as pyang, yanglint, and others allow developers and network engineers to validate, parse, and generate code from YANG models, accelerating development and ensuring compliance with standards. Many vendors also provide APIs that expose their YANG models, allowing for dynamic discovery of available telemetry paths. This capability enables monitoring systems to adapt to device capabilities automatically, eliminating the need for hardcoded queries or manual configuration.

The role of YANG in telemetry is not limited to current device metrics. It also extends to configuration change notifications, state transitions, and event-based triggers. By subscribing to YANG-modeled notifications, collectors can receive alerts when significant events occur, such as link failures, route changes, or configuration updates. This event-driven approach complements traditional telemetry by providing immediate awareness of operational changes, allowing for faster reaction and improved network resilience. Moreover, since these events are defined using the same YANG schema as regular telemetry data, they can be seamlessly integrated into the broader observability pipeline.

YANG data models have fundamentally transformed the way telemetry is implemented and consumed. They provide the structured, vendor-neutral, and extensible framework necessary for high-fidelity network monitoring in today's distributed, multi-vendor environments. By enabling precise data modeling, schema-driven integration, and standardized communication, YANG ensures that telemetry data is both useful and usable across a wide variety of platforms and use cases. As telemetry continues to evolve as a core component of network automation, security, and performance management, the importance of YANG as the language that brings structure and clarity to this data cannot be overstated. Its adoption empowers network operators to achieve greater visibility, consistency, and control, laying the groundwork for smarter, faster, and more reliable infrastructure operations.

Configuring Streaming Telemetry on Routers

Configuring streaming telemetry on routers is an essential task for modern network administrators seeking real-time visibility into the performance and health of their network infrastructure. As networks evolve to support increasing volumes of traffic, more applications, and tighter security requirements, the ability to continuously monitor operational data becomes crucial. Traditional SNMP-based monitoring solutions, which rely on periodic polling, often fail to capture transient events and lack the granularity needed for rapid diagnostics and automated response. Streaming telemetry addresses these shortcomings by allowing routers to push detailed, structured data to collectors at high frequency, enabling more accurate monitoring, faster troubleshooting, and better-informed decision-making. Proper configuration of streaming telemetry on routers involves several steps, including enabling the appropriate telemetry protocols, defining subscriptions, selecting data sources, and configuring transport mechanisms. The process varies slightly across vendors, but the underlying principles remain consistent.

The first step in configuring streaming telemetry on a router is to verify that the device and its software support the desired telemetry features. Most modern routers from leading vendors such as Cisco, Juniper, Arista, and Nokia offer streaming telemetry capabilities through protocols like gRPC with gNMI, NETCONF, or even vendor-specific protocols based on YANG models. Ensuring the router is running a firmware version that includes these capabilities is essential. In some cases, enabling telemetry might require a specific software license or activating a particular feature set. Once support is confirmed, administrators begin by configuring the telemetry agent or sensor on the router, which is responsible for collecting and exporting telemetry data.

At the core of the configuration process is defining telemetry subscriptions. A subscription specifies which data to collect and how often it should be sent. These data points, also known as sensor paths or telemetry paths, are derived from YANG data models that define the structure of device information such as interface statistics, CPU usage, memory metrics, routing table entries, and queue depths. Administrators select relevant paths based on their monitoring objectives. For example, to monitor bandwidth utilization, a subscription might include interface counters like input and output octets. For latency-sensitive applications, the subscription might include buffer occupancy or queuing delay metrics. Subscriptions can be set to operate at regular intervals, known as periodic mode, or event-driven mode, where data is sent only when specific changes occur.

Transport configuration is another critical part of setting up streaming telemetry. Routers need to know where to send the telemetry data and how to do so securely. This typically involves specifying the IP address or hostname of the telemetry collector, the port number for the transport protocol, and any required authentication credentials. Secure transport is often implemented using TLS, with certificates installed on both the router and the collector to establish mutual authentication. Protocols such as gRPC over TLS are widely used for this purpose, providing both performance and security. Some implementations also support failover configurations where multiple collectors can be defined to ensure reliability in case the primary collector becomes unreachable.

Once the subscriptions and transport settings are configured, the router begins exporting telemetry data. This data is sent continuously to the collector in a structured format, typically encoded using Protocol Buffers when gRPC is used. The collector decodes this data, stores it in a time-series database, and makes it available for analysis through dashboards, alerts, or automated workflows. From this point forward, the router plays a passive role, simply sending the requested data as specified by the subscription, while the collector and associated analytics systems perform the heavy lifting of processing, visualizing, and interpreting the information.

Testing and validation are crucial to ensure that the telemetry configuration is working as intended. Network administrators should verify that the telemetry collector is receiving data, that the data matches the expected structure and values, and that the sampling intervals align with the configured settings. Tools such as packet analyzers, CLI show commands, or collector dashboards can be used to confirm that telemetry data is flowing correctly. Additionally, logs should be monitored for errors such as failed connections, dropped packets, or subscription mismatches. In production environments, a misconfigured telemetry session can lead to unnecessary CPU load or excessive traffic, so careful validation helps prevent these issues.

Performance tuning is often required after the initial setup. Depending on the volume of telemetry data being exported and the resources available on the router, administrators may need to adjust the frequency of updates, reduce the number of subscribed paths, or deploy telemetry selectively on critical interfaces rather than across the entire device. Some routers offer rate-limiting features to prevent telemetry traffic from interfering with regular operations. Proper tuning ensures that telemetry delivers useful insights without compromising the performance or stability of the network infrastructure.

Advanced deployments may also include dynamic telemetry configuration, where subscriptions can be modified on the fly by a network controller or automation system. This allows the telemetry system to adapt to changing network conditions, user behavior, or troubleshooting needs. For instance, during a suspected network anomaly, an automation platform could temporarily increase the frequency of telemetry updates for specific metrics or expand the scope of subscriptions to include additional diagnostic data. Once the issue is resolved, the telemetry configuration can be reverted to its baseline state. This flexibility enhances the responsiveness and efficiency of network operations, enabling proactive management rather than reactive firefighting.

Another best practice in configuring telemetry on routers is documenting the telemetry configuration for future reference. This includes recording the sensor paths being used, the transport endpoints, sampling intervals, security settings, and any vendor-specific commands. Documentation facilitates troubleshooting, helps onboard new team members, and ensures consistency across multiple routers and sites. Version control systems can be used to track changes to telemetry configurations over time, providing an audit trail and supporting rollback if needed.

Configuring streaming telemetry on routers represents a shift toward more intelligent, data-driven network management. It transforms routers from passive devices that respond to occasional queries into active participants in a continuous observability ecosystem. When properly configured, telemetry enables real-time monitoring, predictive analytics, and automated remediation, all of which are essential for operating reliable, secure, and high-performance networks. As organizations continue to modernize their infrastructure, telemetry configuration skills will become increasingly important for network engineers, architects, and administrators who are responsible for maintaining operational excellence in the face of growing complexity and demand.

Integrating Telemetry with Analytics Platforms

Integrating telemetry with analytics platforms is a critical step in transforming raw data into actionable intelligence within modern network environments. While streaming telemetry enables devices to continuously export operational metrics, performance indicators, and configuration states, the real value of this data is only realized when it is ingested, processed, and analyzed by powerful analytics platforms capable of deriving insights in real time. The integration process bridges the gap between low-level infrastructure monitoring and high-level business decision-making, allowing organizations to detect anomalies, forecast trends, and automate responses based on real-time network behavior. Achieving effective integration requires a thoughtful approach that considers data normalization, scalability, storage, visualization, and the application of advanced analytics techniques.

The first stage of integrating telemetry with analytics platforms involves setting up data ingestion pipelines. Network devices configured with streaming telemetry push data to collectors using protocols such as gRPC, gNMI, NETCONF, or vendor-specific mechanisms. These collectors act as the entry point to the analytics ecosystem. The raw telemetry data, often encoded in efficient formats like Protocol Buffers, must be decoded and normalized before it can be analyzed. This process ensures that the data conforms to a common structure, regardless of which device or vendor it originated from. Normalization is essential in multi-vendor environments where different devices may express the same metrics using slightly different paths or formats. By mapping all telemetry data to standardized data models, such as OpenConfig YANG schemas, organizations can achieve uniform visibility and simplify downstream processing.

Once the data is normalized, it must be stored in a format suitable for high-volume, high-velocity analysis. Time-series databases are commonly used in telemetry analytics because they are optimized for storing and querying sequences of data points indexed by time. Tools like InfluxDB, Prometheus, and TimescaleDB provide the performance needed to store millions of metrics while supporting complex queries that identify patterns, trends, and thresholds. Some organizations choose to leverage big data platforms like Elasticsearch, Apache Kafka, or Hadoop for additional processing and indexing capabilities. These platforms are particularly useful when telemetry data is combined with other data sources such as logs, events, or configuration changes, creating a more comprehensive view of network operations.

Analytics platforms must be capable of processing large streams of telemetry data in real time. This involves not just storing the data but applying transformations, aggregations, and filters to extract meaningful information. Stream processing engines like Apache Flink, Apache Spark Streaming, and Kafka Streams are commonly integrated with telemetry pipelines to perform real-time analysis on incoming data. These engines can compute moving averages, detect sudden spikes, correlate events, and trigger alerts based on custom logic. For example, if CPU utilization across a group of routers suddenly exceeds a defined threshold while memory usage also spikes, the analytics engine can flag this as a potential failure condition and notify the operations team. By processing telemetry data as it arrives, analytics platforms enable proactive management rather than relying on historical data alone.

Visualization is a vital component of telemetry analytics integration. Dashboards and graphical interfaces allow operators, engineers, and decision-makers to interact with the data in an intuitive way. Tools like

Grafana, Kibana, and Tableau are frequently used to visualize telemetry data through customizable charts, graphs, and heatmaps. These visualizations make it easier to detect outliers, understand trends, and identify problem areas within the network. They also support drill-down capabilities, where users can investigate specific devices, interfaces, or time windows to gain deeper insights. Real-time dashboards that reflect live telemetry data are especially valuable in network operations centers, where visibility into the current state of the network is essential for timely decision-making.

Integrating telemetry with machine learning platforms adds another layer of intelligence to the monitoring system. By feeding telemetry data into models trained to recognize normal and abnormal patterns, organizations can automate the detection of subtle anomalies that might be missed by human observers. These models can predict future performance degradation, identify early indicators of hardware failure, or classify types of traffic that deviate from expected behavior. Telemetry data is ideal for machine learning applications because it is continuous, structured, and inherently time-stamped. Integration with platforms such as TensorFlow, scikit-learn, or cloud-based AI services allows for continuous training, model evaluation, and automated responses. For example, if a model detects an unusual traffic pattern that has historically preceded a DDoS attack, the system can initiate preemptive mitigation strategies before the attack fully materializes.

Automation platforms also benefit significantly from telemetry integration. When telemetry data is used as input to network orchestration and policy engines, the network can respond dynamically to changing conditions. Systems like Ansible, Cisco NSO, or commercial SDN controllers can consume telemetry insights and adjust configurations, reallocate resources, or change routing paths in real time. This closed-loop automation relies on accurate and timely telemetry data to ensure that actions are based on the current state of the network. For instance, if telemetry reveals that a particular link is experiencing high latency and packet loss, the automation engine can reroute critical traffic over a more reliable path without manual intervention. This type of integration enhances network agility and supports self-healing capabilities.

Security analytics is another area where telemetry integration provides significant value. Telemetry data includes a wide range of indicators that can reveal potential security threats, such as unusual port activity, interface errors, configuration changes, or unexpected traffic flows. By correlating telemetry with threat intelligence feeds, firewall logs, and access control lists, security platforms can generate more accurate and contextual alerts. Integrating telemetry into security information and event management systems (SIEM) allows for faster detection of threats and more effective incident response. Furthermore, the detailed operational data captured by telemetry helps forensic analysts reconstruct events after a breach, identify affected systems, and understand how the attack unfolded.

Effective integration also depends on robust APIs and interoperability standards. Analytics platforms must provide well-documented APIs that allow telemetry collectors and third-party tools to ingest data, retrieve insights, and trigger actions. Likewise, telemetry exporters should support standardized protocols and data models that simplify integration. As the telemetry ecosystem matures, support for open standards like OpenConfig, gNMI, and YANG ensures that data can flow freely between devices, collectors, analytics platforms, and automation systems without being locked into proprietary solutions.

Integrating telemetry with analytics platforms transforms raw infrastructure data into operational intelligence. It enables network operators to move beyond static dashboards and threshold-based alerts toward dynamic, predictive, and automated monitoring. This integration empowers organizations to operate their networks more efficiently, respond to issues more quickly, and plan for future needs with greater confidence. The ability to turn real-time telemetry into actionable insights is a fundamental capability for achieving reliability, performance, and security in modern digital infrastructure. As telemetry adoption grows, its integration with analytics platforms will continue to drive innovation and operational excellence across every layer of the network.

Security and Privacy in Telemetry Transmission

Security and privacy in telemetry transmission have become essential concerns as organizations increasingly rely on real-time monitoring to manage their networks, systems, and applications. Telemetry, by its nature, involves the continuous collection and transmission of operational data from devices to centralized collectors or analytics platforms. This data often includes sensitive information about system performance, user activity, traffic patterns, and configuration details. While telemetry enhances visibility, efficiency, and automation, it also introduces new risks. If improperly secured, telemetry channels can become vectors for data leakage, unauthorized access, or manipulation. Ensuring that telemetry transmission is secure and respects privacy requires a multi-layered approach encompassing encryption, authentication, access control, auditing, and careful data governance practices.

One of the foundational pillars of securing telemetry is the encryption of data in transit. Since telemetry data typically traverses IP networks, including public or shared infrastructure, it must be protected against interception and tampering. Modern telemetry protocols such as gRPC and gNMI support encryption through TLS, which ensures that the data is transmitted over a secure channel. TLS not only encrypts the data payload but also validates the identity of the endpoints involved in the communication. Mutual TLS further enhances this by requiring both the device and the collector to authenticate each other using digital certificates. This mutual authentication establishes trust between entities and prevents man-in-the-middle attacks, where an attacker intercepts or alters the data being transmitted between the two parties.

In addition to securing the transport layer, telemetry systems must implement strong authentication and authorization mechanisms. Authentication verifies the identity of telemetry clients and servers, while authorization controls what data can be accessed and by whom. Role-based access control (RBAC) is commonly used in telemetry systems to define different levels of access for administrators, operators, auditors, and third-party systems. For example, an operator might be allowed to view real-time interface statistics but not access configuration change data, while an auditor might have read-only access to historical performance logs. These access controls ensure that telemetry data is not exposed beyond its intended audience and that actions taken within the system are traceable and accountable.

Integrity is another critical aspect of telemetry transmission. It is important to guarantee that the data received by the collector is exactly what was sent by the device, without any modification in transit. Digital signatures and cryptographic hashes can be used to verify the integrity of telemetry messages. When integrity checks are applied, any alteration to the data—whether accidental or malicious—will be detected by the receiving system. This protects against data corruption and supports forensic analysis by ensuring that the telemetry records can be trusted. Many telemetry frameworks include built-in support for integrity verification, which can be configured as part of the data pipeline.

Privacy concerns are particularly relevant in environments where telemetry data might contain user-related information or operational details that could be used to infer confidential activities. For instance, telemetry from a firewall may reveal IP addresses of employees accessing specific services, timestamps of activity, and application usage patterns. In regulated industries such as finance, healthcare, or telecommunications, this type of information may fall under the scope of data protection laws like GDPR, HIPAA, or CCPA. Therefore, telemetry implementations must be designed to minimize the collection of personally identifiable information (PII) and to anonymize or pseudonymize data where appropriate. Anonymization techniques can include the removal or masking of IP addresses, user identifiers, or geographic data. By reducing the granularity of sensitive fields, organizations can preserve privacy without sacrificing operational visibility.

Telemetry systems should also include mechanisms for auditing and logging access to telemetry data. Every interaction with telemetry data—whether it be configuration changes, subscription updates, or data queries—should be recorded with sufficient detail to support traceability and compliance. These audit logs can be used to detect suspicious behavior, investigate incidents, and demonstrate regulatory compliance during audits. Ideally, audit logs themselves should be protected with integrity mechanisms to prevent tampering and should be stored securely in a centralized log management system. Alerts can be configured to notify administrators when unusual access patterns are detected, such as attempts to subscribe to restricted telemetry paths or repeated authentication failures.

Network segmentation and firewall policies also play a role in securing telemetry transmission. Telemetry traffic should be isolated from general user traffic and restricted to known, trusted paths between devices and collectors. This limits the exposure of telemetry data to internal threats and reduces the risk of lateral movement in the event of a breach. Using virtual private networks or encrypted tunnels can further safeguard telemetry traffic, especially when it must traverse untrusted networks or connect multiple sites across a wide-area network. In cloud environments, security groups and identity-based access policies should be applied to virtual telemetry agents and collectors to enforce strict communication boundaries.

Vendor-specific telemetry implementations must be evaluated carefully to ensure they adhere to security best practices. Some proprietary telemetry protocols may lack modern encryption or authentication features, relying instead on legacy mechanisms or assuming that the network is inherently secure. In such cases, organizations should push vendors to adopt open standards like OpenConfig, gNMI, and YANG models, which support secure telemetry by design. Additionally, organizations should perform regular security assessments of their telemetry infrastructure, including penetration testing, code reviews, and configuration audits. This helps identify vulnerabilities and misconfigurations before they can be exploited by attackers.

Telemetry retention policies are also important for maintaining security and privacy. Organizations must define how long telemetry data is stored, where it is stored, and who has access to it. Retaining data longer than necessary increases the risk of exposure in the event of a breach. Conversely, overly aggressive data purging can limit the effectiveness of analytics and hinder investigations. A balanced retention policy, aligned with business requirements and regulatory obligations, should be enforced through data lifecycle management tools. Encryption at rest should be applied to stored telemetry data, ensuring that even if the storage medium is compromised, the data remains unreadable without proper decryption keys.

Education and awareness are essential components of securing telemetry transmission. Network engineers, developers, and security teams must be trained on the risks associated with telemetry data and the proper use of telemetry tools. Clear policies should define acceptable use, data classification, and response procedures in the event of a telemetry-related incident. As telemetry becomes more deeply integrated with automation and decision-making processes, the potential impact of compromised telemetry data grows. Ensuring that everyone involved understands their role in maintaining telemetry security helps build a resilient and trustworthy monitoring system.

Securing and protecting the privacy of telemetry transmission is a multidimensional challenge that requires careful attention to protocol selection, transport security, access control, data minimization, and auditing. As telemetry becomes more integral to network operations and decision-making, organizations must adopt a holistic approach to safeguarding the data it generates and transmits. By implementing strong security practices and maintaining a culture of privacy awareness, it is possible to leverage the full benefits of telemetry while mitigating the risks it introduces. The success of a telemetry system depends not only on its technical capabilities but also on the robustness of the security framework that supports it.

Monitoring Network Health with Telemetry

Monitoring network health with telemetry has become an indispensable practice in managing today's complex, dynamic, and high-performing network environments. Traditional monitoring approaches based on periodic polling, log analysis, and manual inspection are no longer sufficient for organizations that require constant visibility, instant feedback, and proactive remediation. Telemetry provides a real-time, granular, and continuous view into network operations, allowing engineers and administrators to observe performance metrics, detect anomalies, and maintain service quality at scale. By enabling devices to push structured data to centralized collectors, telemetry reduces the latency and blind spots associated with legacy tools and lays the groundwork for intelligent, automated network management.

One of the primary advantages of using telemetry to monitor network health is the ability to track critical performance indicators in near real time. These include interface utilization, CPU and memory usage, packet loss, jitter, latency, buffer occupancy, and routing state changes. With telemetry, these metrics are no longer sampled at coarse intervals but are streamed continuously, offering far more detailed insight into the behavior of the network. This enhanced visibility allows administrators to detect subtle performance degradations before they evolve into service-impacting outages. For example, a growing trend in interface queue depth might signal an impending congestion issue, prompting preventive actions such as traffic rerouting or capacity adjustments.

Another vital function of telemetry in network health monitoring is the correlation of disparate data points to identify root causes. In large-scale environments, a single issue can ripple across multiple layers of the network and affect numerous systems. Telemetry provides the contextual data needed to understand these relationships. When a drop in throughput is observed, telemetry can reveal whether it coincides with an increase in CPU load on a router, a spike in retransmissions, or a configuration change pushed to a firewall. By piecing together these clues, engineers can isolate the true cause of a problem and resolve it faster. This reduces mean time to resolution and minimizes the operational impact of performance issues.

Telemetry also supports the continuous validation of network policies and configurations. Modern networks often rely on segmentation, quality of service, access controls, and routing policies to enforce security and ensure performance. Telemetry allows operators to verify that these policies are functioning as intended. For example, telemetry data might show whether specific applications are receiving their designated bandwidth, whether routing paths are changing unexpectedly, or whether ACLs are inadvertently blocking critical traffic. These insights allow for fine-tuning of configurations and help ensure that network behavior aligns with design intent. This is particularly important in dynamic environments where configuration drift and unintended consequences can arise from frequent changes.

Proactive maintenance is another area where telemetry plays a significant role in preserving network health. Devices inevitably experience wear, software bugs, and capacity constraints. Telemetry enables early detection of hardware degradation or resource exhaustion by continuously monitoring environmental conditions and operational metrics. A pattern of increasing CRC errors on an interface, rising fan speeds, or memory fragmentation could signal the need for preemptive maintenance or component replacement. By addressing these issues before they lead to failures, organizations can maintain high availability and reduce the likelihood of unexpected outages.

Capacity planning and network optimization are also enhanced through telemetry-based monitoring. As organizations grow and traffic patterns evolve, maintaining a healthy network requires foresight and data-driven planning. Telemetry provides long-term visibility into bandwidth consumption, application usage trends, and growth trajectories. By analyzing this data, network teams can forecast demand, identify underutilized or overburdened links, and plan upgrades accordingly. This strategic insight supports smarter investment decisions and ensures that infrastructure scales in step with organizational needs. Instead of reacting to congestion or bottlenecks after they occur, telemetry empowers teams to build networks that are resilient, efficient, and future-proof.

Telemetry further contributes to service assurance and user experience monitoring. Network performance is ultimately measured by how well it supports applications and users. Telemetry makes it possible to monitor application-specific traffic, assess path performance, and detect anomalies at the service level. For instance, if users report slow access to a cloud-based application, telemetry can help determine whether the issue lies in the WAN connection, the internal switching fabric, or the application itself. This end-to-end visibility is crucial in hybrid and multi-cloud environments where the network spans diverse technologies and administrative domains. By maintaining continuous insight into service performance, organizations can uphold service-level agreements and deliver consistent user experiences.

Security monitoring also benefits from telemetry's role in assessing network health. Many security threats manifest as changes in normal traffic behavior, unexpected system activity, or anomalies in usage patterns. Telemetry captures the operational context in which these anomalies occur, providing valuable input for threat detection systems. For example, telemetry might detect a sudden increase in outbound traffic from a single host, a sharp rise in failed login attempts, or unexpected protocol usage. These indicators, when correlated with other security data, can point to compromised systems, insider threats, or misconfigurations. By incorporating telemetry into the security monitoring framework, organizations gain an additional layer of defense and insight.

Another critical element of telemetry in network health monitoring is automation readiness. Telemetry provides the real-time feedback needed for closed-loop automation systems, which adjust network behavior based on current conditions. For example, if telemetry detects that a particular link is experiencing high latency, the automation platform can dynamically reroute traffic to an alternative path. If device resources are nearing exhaustion, load balancing actions can be initiated. These feedback-driven adjustments help maintain optimal performance and reduce the operational burden on human administrators. Over time, such systems can learn from telemetry data to improve their decision-making, enabling self-optimizing networks that adapt to changing conditions without manual intervention.

The deployment of telemetry for network health monitoring requires a thoughtful approach to architecture and configuration. Devices must be equipped with telemetry agents capable of exporting relevant metrics, and collectors must be provisioned to ingest, normalize, and store this data. Analytics platforms must be configured to generate meaningful insights, and visualization tools must present this information in intuitive formats for operators. Subscription models should be carefully defined to ensure that the right data is collected without overwhelming the system. Sampling intervals, data formats, transport protocols, and security settings all play a role in ensuring that telemetry data is accurate, timely, and secure.

Monitoring network health with telemetry represents a significant advancement in the way organizations manage their infrastructure. It transforms networks from opaque systems into observable environments where data flows continuously, enabling visibility that is immediate, comprehensive, and actionable. As networks become more critical to business operations, more distributed, and more complex, the ability to monitor their health through telemetry becomes not just a best practice but a necessity. It enables teams to move from reactive troubleshooting to proactive management, supporting higher availability, better performance, and more efficient operations. With the right telemetry framework in place, organizations can maintain robust, resilient, and intelligent networks that meet the demands of the modern digital world.

Performance Metrics and KPI Tracking

Performance metrics and KPI tracking form the foundation of effective network monitoring, operations, and long-term planning. In a world increasingly dependent on high-performing digital infrastructure, organizations cannot afford to operate their networks without real-time and historical visibility into key indicators of service quality, system performance, and operational efficiency. These metrics not only serve as tools for immediate troubleshooting but also support trend analysis, capacity planning, SLA enforcement, and strategic decision-making. With the rise of telemetry as a primary data collection method, the accuracy, granularity, and timeliness of performance metrics have improved dramatically, giving network administrators and business leaders a powerful set of tools to evaluate the health and success of network services.

The first step in tracking performance metrics is identifying what to measure. Not all data points are equally valuable, and it is essential to focus on those metrics that directly impact network performance and user experience. These include bandwidth utilization, packet loss, latency, jitter, CPU and memory usage, interface error rates, throughput, and availability. Each of these indicators offers insight into a different dimension of network performance. For example, high bandwidth utilization may suggest congestion, while increased packet loss could point to physical layer issues or misconfigured queuing policies. Monitoring these metrics at fine time intervals allows operations teams to detect problems early and respond before they escalate.

Latency is one of the most important metrics for real-time applications such as voice, video, and financial trading. Even small increases in delay can have significant impacts on performance and user experience. Telemetry allows for continuous measurement of latency across different segments of the network, helping engineers identify bottlenecks and reroute traffic if necessary. Similarly, jitter—the variation in packet delay—is critical for understanding the quality of interactive sessions. Consistent jitter can degrade voice calls or video conferencing even when average latency appears acceptable. By tracking jitter over time, organizations can optimize queuing policies and traffic engineering to stabilize performance for time-sensitive applications.

Packet loss is another key metric that directly correlates with service degradation. Whether caused by interface congestion, faulty hardware, or corrupted data streams, packet loss affects throughput and reliability. Telemetry allows for detailed packet loss tracking per interface, per device, or even per application, depending on the granularity of the data collected. When analyzed alongside other metrics, packet loss patterns can reveal underlying issues such as failing links or saturated buffers. Continuous loss tracking also enables organizations to maintain compliance with SLAs that specify minimum service quality thresholds.

Throughput measurements help assess how effectively a network is carrying data over time. This metric is essential for validating whether infrastructure investments are delivering expected performance gains. It also helps in identifying asymmetries in traffic flows, which may indicate routing issues or application behavior that requires tuning. Telemetry-based throughput monitoring allows for real-time analysis and comparison across multiple links, interfaces, or service paths, supporting balanced network usage and efficient resource allocation.

CPU and memory usage metrics are critical for understanding the internal health of network devices. Routers, switches, firewalls, and load balancers all rely on adequate system resources to perform their functions. Telemetry provides continuous visibility into how these resources are consumed, allowing teams to detect spikes, leaks, or saturation events that could lead to degraded performance or outages. This information supports both short-term incident resolution and long-term capacity planning, ensuring that devices remain within safe operating thresholds.

Availability is perhaps the most foundational metric in any network environment. It refers to the ability of a service or device to remain operational and reachable over time. High availability is often measured as a percentage, representing uptime over a defined period. For critical services, organizations may require availability targets of 99.99 percent or higher. Telemetry helps track availability at multiple levels, from individual device uptime to service-level reachability. When outages occur, telemetry data can be used to pinpoint the time of failure, the scope of impact, and the duration of the event, all of which are vital for root cause analysis and SLA reporting.

Tracking key performance indicators (KPIs) involves aggregating and analyzing performance metrics in ways that align with business goals and operational priorities. While raw metrics are valuable, KPIs provide higher-level insights that reflect the overall success of network initiatives. Examples of KPIs include average application response time, percentage of successful transactions, mean time to detect incidents, and mean time to resolve problems. These indicators allow leadership teams to measure how well the network supports organizational objectives and where improvements are needed.

Automation plays an increasing role in KPI tracking. With the volume of telemetry data generated by modern networks, manual analysis is no longer feasible. Analytics platforms ingest telemetry streams, calculate KPIs in real time, and present the results in dashboards tailored to different audiences. Operations teams receive alerts when KPIs fall below defined thresholds, while executives access summary views that highlight trends and performance over time. Predictive analytics can also be applied to KPIs, enabling proactive resource allocation, risk mitigation, and investment planning based on projected needs.

Historical KPI tracking is equally important for identifying trends, setting benchmarks, and validating the impact of infrastructure changes. For instance, an organization that upgrades its WAN links can use pre- and post-upgrade KPI comparisons to assess whether the investment yielded measurable improvements. Similarly, trend analysis can reveal gradual degradations that may not trigger immediate alerts but signal the need for preventative maintenance or configuration adjustments.

The integration of KPIs into service level agreements formalizes performance expectations between internal teams or with external customers. SLAs define acceptable ranges for specific KPIs and establish penalties or escalation procedures when targets are not met. Telemetry-based KPI tracking ensures that SLA compliance can be verified with precision and transparency. This fosters accountability, builds trust, and provides objective data to resolve disputes or renegotiate terms.

Effective performance metrics and KPI tracking also support incident postmortems and continuous improvement efforts. After an outage or performance degradation, detailed telemetry data enables teams to reconstruct the sequence of events, identify contributing factors, and determine corrective actions. Documenting the impact on KPIs provides a quantifiable view of the incident's severity and informs the prioritization of remediation efforts.

Ultimately, performance metrics and KPI tracking enable organizations to transform raw telemetry data into strategic intelligence. By focusing on meaningful indicators and maintaining accurate, real-time visibility into network conditions, teams can ensure consistent service delivery, maintain compliance, and drive continuous improvement. As networks continue to grow in complexity and criticality, the importance of robust KPI frameworks will only increase, forming the backbone of a data-driven approach to network operations and business alignment.

Comparative Analysis of SNMP, NetFlow, sFlow, and Telemetry

In the modern networking landscape, monitoring and managing network performance, security, and reliability have become paramount as organizations depend on complex infrastructures to support their operations. Over the years, a variety of protocols and methods have been developed to facilitate network monitoring, each with its own strengths, weaknesses, and use cases. Four of the most widely adopted approaches to network monitoring are SNMP (Simple Network Management Protocol), NetFlow, sFlow, and Telemetry. While all these methods offer valuable insights into network health, they operate in fundamentally different ways and are suited to different types of environments and objectives.

SNMP, one of the oldest and most widely used network monitoring protocols, relies on a client-server architecture where a central network management system (NMS) periodically polls devices to gather status information such as interface statistics, device uptime, and error counts. SNMP operates in a request-response model where an NMS sends requests to network devices, and the devices respond with the requested data. Although SNMP is simple to deploy and widely supported by network devices, it has limitations when it comes to real-time visibility and scalability. The protocol is inherently pull-based, meaning the NMS is responsible for initiating communication with the network device at regular intervals. As a result, there are inherent delays in capturing data, and because of this polling mechanism, SNMP may miss transient events or short-lived problems that could have a significant impact on network performance. Furthermore, SNMP does not provide a very detailed view of network traffic patterns or application behavior, focusing primarily on system-level statistics rather than the flow of data across the network.

NetFlow, developed by Cisco, takes a more detailed and flow-based approach to network monitoring. Rather than periodically polling devices for status updates, NetFlow collects information about network traffic flows. A flow in NetFlow terminology refers to a set of packets that share common attributes such as source and destination IP addresses, ports, and protocols. NetFlow captures metadata about these flows and aggregates this data into flow records, which are then sent to a collector for analysis. NetFlow provides deeper insights into network traffic than SNMP, including visibility into which applications and users are consuming bandwidth, which paths traffic is taking through the network, and how network resources are being utilized. This detailed flow data makes NetFlow particularly useful for network performance monitoring, troubleshooting, and capacity planning. However, like SNMP, NetFlow relies on a pull-based approach, which can introduce latency in data collection, and it does not offer continuous visibility or support for real-time analysis. Additionally, because NetFlow records are based on flow aggregation, there is still some loss of granularity compared to direct packet-level monitoring.

sFlow, in contrast, takes a more efficient and scalable approach by using statistical sampling rather than capturing all flow data. sFlow samples packets at regular intervals and sends these samples to a central collector. This method significantly reduces the volume of data that needs to be processed, making sFlow highly scalable and well-suited for large networks with high-speed links. Unlike NetFlow, which captures flow data for all traffic passing through a device, sFlow provides a representative sample of the traffic and can offer insights into a broad range of traffic types, including unicast, multicast, and broadcast traffic. This makes sFlow particularly useful in large, high-performance environments where capturing every packet would overwhelm the device and the monitoring system. While sFlow provides a more efficient means of monitoring large networks, the trade-off is that sampled data may not provide as much precision as NetFlow or other flow-based solutions. Events that occur between sampling intervals may go unnoticed, and while statistical methods can estimate traffic behavior, the accuracy of these estimates depends on the sampling rate and the randomness of the packet selection.

Telemetry, on the other hand, represents the next evolution in network monitoring. Unlike SNMP, NetFlow, and sFlow, which are based on periodic polling or sampling, telemetry enables continuous, real-time data streaming from devices to collectors. Telemetry allows devices to push operational data such as interface counters, CPU usage, memory usage, and more to centralized collectors without waiting for queries. This push-based model provides much lower latency compared to polling systems, offering near-instantaneous visibility into network state and performance. Furthermore, telemetry supports a wide range of data types, including detailed, time-series data that can be used for predictive analytics, machine learning, and automation. With telemetry, network operators can monitor a vast array of metrics and take corrective actions based on real-time data. Telemetry-based solutions also often integrate with modern analytics platforms, enabling advanced features such as anomaly detection, trend analysis, and automated decision-making based on the current network state.

The key advantage of telemetry is its ability to provide continuous visibility with very low latency, which makes it ideal for environments where real-time monitoring is critical, such as in financial trading, VoIP networks, or large data centers. Additionally, telemetry allows for much more granular and flexible data collection compared to SNMP and flow-based solutions. It supports a wide variety of data sources, including performance metrics, logs, and environmental data, and it allows devices to export data at customizable intervals or based on specific events or thresholds. This flexibility enables operators to fine-tune their monitoring systems to focus on the most relevant data for their use cases. However, the adoption of telemetry requires more advanced infrastructure and configuration compared to SNMP or NetFlow, as it involves setting up real-time streaming pipelines and ensuring the correct data is being captured and transmitted.

While each of these monitoring methods has its strengths and weaknesses, the choice between them largely depends on the specific needs of the network and the goals of the monitoring system. SNMP remains a good option for basic health monitoring and simple device management, especially in environments where legacy systems and cost constraints are a consideration. NetFlow is highly effective in environments where understanding detailed traffic flows is essential, and it is particularly useful for monitoring bandwidth consumption, troubleshooting congestion issues, and performing traffic analysis. sFlow excels in large-scale, high-speed networks where scalability and efficiency are paramount, offering a good balance between visibility and resource consumption. Telemetry, with its real-time, continuous data stream, is ideal for environments where immediate response, predictive analytics, and automation are critical. It is particularly suited to next-generation networks that require real-time monitoring, automation, and integration with advanced analytics platforms.

Ultimately, many modern networks benefit from a combination of these technologies, leveraging SNMP for simple device health checks, NetFlow or sFlow for traffic monitoring, and telemetry for real-time, granular insights into network performance. By integrating these monitoring methods, organizations can build a comprehensive, multi-layered monitoring system that supports proactive management, operational efficiency, and long-term planning.

Choosing the Right Protocol for the Job

Choosing the right protocol for network monitoring and telemetry is a decision that directly impacts an organization's ability to maintain optimal network performance, ensure security, and make data-driven decisions. With a variety of protocols available, each offering unique capabilities, understanding the strengths, weaknesses, and ideal use cases of each protocol is crucial. The decision-making process involves evaluating factors such as scalability, granularity of data, real-time capabilities, network infrastructure, and the specific monitoring goals. Whether using SNMP, NetFlow, sFlow, or telemetry, the choice of protocol will dictate how effectively the network can be managed and how well the monitoring system can adapt to evolving business and technological demands.

The first consideration when selecting a protocol is the level of detail required for monitoring. For many basic network monitoring needs, SNMP is often the starting point. SNMP, as one of the oldest and most widely supported protocols, offers simplicity and broad compatibility. It allows network devices to expose performance metrics, such as interface statistics, device health, and error counts. While SNMP's polling-based approach provides periodic snapshots of a device's status, it lacks the granularity needed for more detailed traffic analysis or real-time performance monitoring. For environments where detailed insights into traffic flow, bandwidth usage, and application performance are critical, more specialized protocols such as NetFlow or sFlow may be necessary.

NetFlow is highly effective when granular traffic data is required. By capturing flow data, NetFlow enables network operators to track the flow of traffic between devices, identify bottlenecks, and gain a better understanding of how applications utilize the network. It is especially useful in environments where traffic patterns need to be analyzed for capacity planning, troubleshooting, or security monitoring. However, NetFlow has limitations in terms of real-time monitoring, as it primarily collects data at intervals and does not offer continuous visibility. NetFlow is also inherently more resource-intensive than SNMP due to the aggregation and export of flow records. In high-throughput networks, NetFlow can create significant overhead on devices, particularly if flow export is not optimized.

On the other hand, sFlow provides an alternative approach by using statistical sampling to collect data about traffic. sFlow captures packet-level data at regular intervals, offering a more scalable solution for high-speed networks. Unlike NetFlow, sFlow does not collect flow records for every individual conversation, making it much more efficient in terms of resource usage. This efficiency makes sFlow ideal for large-scale networks where it is impractical to capture every flow or for environments with high-speed links, such as data centers and service provider networks. While sFlow offers a less detailed view compared to NetFlow, it provides a good balance between visibility and performance, especially in environments where general traffic patterns and aggregate performance metrics are sufficient.

However, when network monitoring requirements evolve and real-time, continuous visibility becomes a priority, telemetry stands out as the ideal solution. Telemetry, particularly in the context of modern SDN (Software-Defined Networking) and cloud-native environments, allows for the streaming of data directly from devices to collectors in near real-time. Unlike SNMP, NetFlow, or sFlow, telemetry eliminates the need for periodic polling or sampling by pushing data to collectors continuously. This push-based model offers immediate insights into network performance and can be leveraged for predictive analytics, anomaly detection, and automated responses to network events. The ability to monitor a wide array of metrics, from hardware resource utilization to traffic patterns and device configurations, makes telemetry an invaluable tool for organizations that require detailed, real-time insights into their network infrastructure.

Scalability is another key factor to consider when choosing a protocol. For small to medium-sized networks with relatively simple monitoring needs, SNMP may be sufficient. Its minimal resource requirements and ease of implementation make it a cost-effective option for organizations just starting to build their monitoring capabilities. However, as networks grow in complexity and size, SNMP may begin to show its limitations in terms of visibility and data granularity. NetFlow and sFlow are better suited for larger networks, where monitoring needs shift toward more detailed traffic analysis and performance optimization. NetFlow's ability to capture flow data and sFlow's statistical sampling both offer more scalability than SNMP by reducing the overhead involved in collecting and processing data.

In contrast, telemetry shines in highly dynamic and large-scale environments, such as cloud environments or modern data centers. The ability to stream data continuously from thousands of devices or virtualized instances without creating significant bottlenecks is a key advantage of telemetry. Telemetry's efficiency in real-time monitoring, combined with its capability to scale with the size and complexity of the network, makes it the preferred protocol for organizations that need to monitor constantly evolving infrastructures with minimal latency and high precision. However, implementing telemetry requires a more sophisticated infrastructure and more complex configuration than SNMP, NetFlow, or sFlow.

Security is another important consideration in protocol selection. As organizations collect more data and increase visibility into their networks, the risk of exposing sensitive information grows. SNMP, especially older versions like SNMPv1 and SNMPv2c, are known to have security vulnerabilities, such as weak authentication mechanisms and lack of encryption. This makes SNMP unsuitable for environments where security is a top priority. In contrast, newer protocols like NetFlow, sFlow, and telemetry, especially when used with secure transport protocols such as TLS, offer stronger encryption and authentication mechanisms, ensuring the confidentiality and integrity of telemetry data. When selecting a protocol, organizations must assess the security requirements of their network and ensure that the protocol chosen supports secure communication, especially if sensitive operational data is being transmitted.

Another aspect to consider is the compatibility and integration with other network management and analytics platforms. SNMP has been the de facto standard for network management and is supported by nearly all network devices. This broad support makes it a convenient choice for basic monitoring, but it can fall short when it comes to integration with more modern analytics or automation platforms. NetFlow and sFlow, on the other hand, integrate well with traffic analysis tools, security platforms, and performance monitoring solutions. Telemetry, due to its flexibility and real-time data streaming capabilities, is well-suited for integration with advanced analytics platforms, machine learning systems, and automation engines, which are increasingly becoming standard in modern IT environments.

Ultimately, choosing the right protocol for network monitoring depends on the specific needs of the organization, the scale of the network, the level of detail required, and the need for real-time insights. For basic monitoring in small environments, SNMP may be sufficient. For traffic and performance analysis, NetFlow or sFlow offer more detailed insights with lower resource overhead than SNMP. When real-time, continuous visibility is required, especially in large-scale, dynamic environments, telemetry provides a comprehensive and scalable solution. By carefully assessing the requirements, organizations can choose the protocol that best aligns with their operational goals and network management strategy, ensuring that their infrastructure is effectively monitored, secure, and optimized for performance.

Hybrid Monitoring Architectures

As networks evolve to meet the increasing demands of businesses and the integration of diverse technologies, the need for comprehensive, scalable, and efficient network monitoring solutions has become critical. Organizations today rely on complex, hybrid environments that combine on-premises infrastructure, cloud services, and virtualized resources. These hybrid environments present unique challenges for network monitoring, as they span multiple platforms, vendors, and architectures, often leading to silos of data and limited visibility. Hybrid monitoring architectures have emerged as a solution to address these challenges by integrating diverse monitoring technologies and data sources into a unified system, providing real-time, end-to-end visibility across both physical and virtual network elements.

A hybrid monitoring architecture is designed to bridge the gap between traditional on-premises monitoring systems and cloud-native tools, allowing for seamless integration of data from different network domains. This approach is necessary because networks no longer operate solely within the confines of a single physical location. Today, businesses use a combination of on-premises data centers, public and private clouds, remote offices, and edge computing devices to deliver services. Each of these elements often requires its own monitoring solution, which can lead to fragmented visibility and inefficient management. A hybrid monitoring architecture consolidates data from all of these sources, offering a holistic view of the network and ensuring that organizations can manage performance, troubleshoot issues, and maintain security across the entire infrastructure.

At the core of a hybrid monitoring architecture is the integration of multiple monitoring tools and protocols. These may include traditional monitoring solutions like SNMP, NetFlow, and sFlow, as well as more modern telemetry-based systems that provide continuous, real-time data. These protocols are designed to operate in different environments, and by combining them, organizations can leverage the strengths of each. For example, SNMP may be used for basic device health monitoring on legacy equipment, while telemetry is used to stream real-time performance data from cloud-based resources and virtualized environments. NetFlow or sFlow can be utilized for deep traffic analysis, while telemetry captures detailed, application-specific metrics. By integrating these monitoring methods, a hybrid architecture allows organizations to maintain visibility over both their legacy and next-generation network components.

The ability to integrate cloud-based monitoring tools is another key feature of hybrid architectures. Cloud providers like AWS, Microsoft Azure, and Google Cloud offer their own set of monitoring tools, which provide valuable insights into cloud infrastructure performance. These tools can track metrics such as virtual machine health, storage usage, and network performance within the cloud environment. However, monitoring solutions for cloud infrastructures often operate independently of on-premises systems, creating a fragmented view of the overall network. Hybrid monitoring architectures address this issue by integrating cloud monitoring data into the central monitoring platform. This integration enables administrators to correlate data from cloud-based services with data from on-premises systems, providing a comprehensive view of the entire network, regardless of location.

A crucial aspect of hybrid monitoring is the centralized collection and analysis of telemetry data. Telemetry provides continuous, real-time data streams from network devices, applications, and services. Unlike traditional polling-based systems, telemetry sends data as it changes, which allows for immediate detection of network issues. The integration of telemetry in a hybrid monitoring architecture enables organizations to capture performance data from both on-premises and cloud environments in real time. This is particularly important for organizations with dynamic, rapidly changing networks, as it allows for proactive identification of performance degradation, security threats, and configuration drift. By consolidating telemetry data from all parts of the network into a central analytics platform, administrators can gain deeper insights into network health and performance, improving their ability to respond to issues as they arise.

The use of artificial intelligence (AI) and machine learning (ML) is another benefit of hybrid monitoring architectures. With the vast amounts of data generated by modern networks, manual analysis becomes impractical. AI and ML algorithms can be used to process telemetry data, detect anomalies, and predict future performance trends. For instance, by analyzing historical performance data, these algorithms can identify patterns that indicate potential issues, such as bandwidth congestion, server overloads, or security threats. The ability to predict and address problems before they impact users is one of the key advantages of integrating AI and ML into hybrid monitoring architectures. These tools can also help optimize network performance by recommending configuration changes or resource reallocations based on real-time data analysis.

Security is a paramount concern in any network monitoring solution, especially in hybrid environments where data is transmitted across both private and public networks. Hybrid monitoring architectures must incorporate robust security measures to protect sensitive telemetry data. This includes encrypting data in transit, implementing access control mechanisms to restrict who can view or modify telemetry data, and ensuring that all monitoring systems comply with relevant security policies and regulations. In addition, hybrid architectures should integrate with security information and event management (SIEM) systems, which aggregate and analyze security-related data from across the network. This integration allows for real-time detection of security incidents, such as unauthorized access attempts or abnormal traffic patterns that may indicate a security breach.

One of the key challenges of implementing a hybrid monitoring architecture is ensuring that the data from different sources is consistent and can be easily correlated. With multiple monitoring tools in use, there is often a risk that data will be siloed or formatted in incompatible ways. To address this, many hybrid monitoring architectures leverage common data standards, such as OpenConfig and YANG, which define how telemetry data should be structured and transmitted. By using these standardized data models, organizations can ensure that data from different vendors, platforms, and environments can be integrated seamlessly. Additionally, the use of application programming interfaces (APIs) is essential for enabling data exchange between monitoring tools, ensuring that all relevant data is brought together into a single, unified platform for analysis.

Scalability is another important consideration for hybrid monitoring architectures. As networks grow and become more complex, the monitoring solution must be able to scale to handle the increased data volume and diversity. Hybrid architectures that rely on cloud-based monitoring tools and distributed data collection can scale more easily than traditional on-premises solutions. Cloud infrastructure allows for elastic scaling, meaning that resources can be dynamically allocated based on demand. This makes hybrid monitoring architectures particularly well-suited to modern, cloud-first environments where workloads and network demands can fluctuate dramatically.

In summary, hybrid monitoring architectures provide a powerful solution for organizations that need to monitor diverse and complex network environments. By integrating multiple monitoring tools and protocols, including SNMP, NetFlow, sFlow, and telemetry, these architectures offer comprehensive, real-time visibility across both on-premises and cloud-based resources. They also leverage AI and ML to automate data analysis and prediction, while ensuring robust security and compliance. As networks continue to grow in size and complexity, hybrid monitoring will play an increasingly important role in helping organizations maintain network health, optimize performance, and secure their infrastructures.

Data Storage and Retention Strategies

Data storage and retention strategies are critical components of modern network management and enterprise IT infrastructure. As organizations generate and collect increasing amounts of data, particularly from network devices, telemetry systems, and monitoring platforms, it becomes essential to implement well-structured and efficient strategies for storing and retaining this data. The decisions made around data storage and retention not only impact how information is accessed and used but also play a crucial role in ensuring compliance with regulations, optimizing performance, managing costs, and supporting long-term business objectives. With the rapid expansion of network monitoring and telemetry technologies, it is important to understand the various considerations that go into shaping data storage and retention strategies, as well as the challenges and best practices associated with these processes.

One of the fundamental considerations in data storage is the choice of storage infrastructure. The two primary options for storing large volumes of data are on-premises storage and cloud storage. On-premises storage offers full control over data management, including hardware and security measures, but it often requires significant capital investment in infrastructure and ongoing maintenance costs. It may also have limitations in terms of scalability, making it less suitable for organizations with growing data needs or dynamic workloads. In contrast, cloud storage provides a more flexible, scalable solution that can accommodate large volumes of data without the need for heavy upfront investments. Many cloud providers offer services optimized for storing time-series data, making them particularly well-suited for network telemetry and monitoring systems. Cloud storage, however, introduces concerns about data privacy, security, and compliance, especially when sensitive data crosses geographical boundaries or is stored in shared environments.

When implementing data storage solutions, it is crucial to consider the type of data being stored and its intended use. Different types of data have varying storage and retention needs based on factors such as access frequency, size, and sensitivity. For example, real-time network monitoring data such as latency, packet loss, and bandwidth utilization may need to be stored in a way that allows for quick retrieval and analysis. These data points are often time-sensitive and require a fast storage solution, such as solid-state drives (SSDs), which provide low-latency access. On the other hand, historical data or logs that may only be accessed occasionally for troubleshooting or compliance purposes can be stored on slower, more cost-effective media, such as hard disk drives (HDDs) or cold storage in the cloud. Understanding the nature of different data types and their access patterns is critical to optimizing storage costs while ensuring performance.

Data retention strategies are just as important as the storage solutions themselves. Retention policies dictate how long data should be stored and when it should be deleted or archived. Retaining data indefinitely can lead to storage bloat and unnecessary costs, while insufficient retention periods may result in lost data that could be valuable for troubleshooting, trend analysis, or regulatory compliance. A well-defined retention policy takes into account both the business needs of the organization and any legal or regulatory requirements. For instance, financial institutions may be required to retain certain types of data for several years, while other less critical data may be safely deleted or archived after a shorter period. Additionally, organizations must be mindful of data privacy regulations such as the General Data Protection Regulation (GDPR) or the California Consumer Privacy Act (CCPA), which set limits on data retention and require organizations to ensure that personal data is not stored longer than necessary.

Archiving is an important part of data retention strategy, especially for data that is infrequently accessed but still needs to be preserved for compliance or historical reference. Archiving involves moving data from primary storage to secondary, lower-cost storage systems, typically in the cloud or on offline media. This reduces the load on active storage while still ensuring that data can be retrieved when needed. The key challenge with archiving is ensuring that archived data remains accessible and retrievable in a usable format. This requires careful consideration of file formats, indexing, and metadata management to ensure that the archived data remains searchable and compatible with future analytics tools.

To support data retention and archiving, many organizations implement tiered storage strategies. Tiered storage involves categorizing data based on its frequency of use and its value, then placing it on different types of storage media accordingly. For example, frequently accessed real-time data may be stored on high-performance SSDs, while less frequently accessed historical data is moved to cheaper, slower storage tiers. This approach balances the need for fast access to critical data with the goal of minimizing storage costs. Furthermore, automated tiering systems can help ensure that data is moved to the appropriate storage tier without manual intervention, reducing administrative overhead and ensuring efficient data management.

Data compression and deduplication techniques are also important tools for optimizing storage and retention. Compression reduces the size of stored data by removing redundant information, making it possible to store more data in less space. Deduplication, on the other hand, identifies and eliminates duplicate copies of data, ensuring that only unique data is stored. These techniques are particularly valuable in environments with large volumes of time-series data, such as network monitoring or telemetry systems, where a significant amount of data may be redundant across multiple devices or monitoring intervals. By using compression and deduplication, organizations can significantly reduce storage costs while maintaining access to all the necessary data.

Another consideration when developing data storage and retention strategies is the need for regular backups and disaster recovery plans. Backup systems ensure that data is replicated and can be restored in case of hardware failure, cyberattack, or natural disaster. For mission-critical data, organizations often implement real-time or near-real-time backup systems that ensure minimal data loss. Disaster recovery plans should also include provisions for restoring archived data and ensuring that backup systems are regularly tested and updated. With the increasing reliance on data-driven decision-making, having a robust data backup and recovery plan is essential to ensuring business continuity and protecting valuable information.

Finally, governance and auditing are critical components of data storage and retention strategies. Effective data governance ensures that data is managed in a way that aligns with organizational policies, regulatory requirements, and industry standards. This includes managing access controls, ensuring data integrity, and tracking data usage. Auditing mechanisms help ensure compliance with data retention policies by monitoring access and modifications to stored data. By implementing comprehensive governance and auditing frameworks, organizations can reduce the risk of non-compliance and ensure that data retention practices align with industry best practices and legal requirements.

In an era of rapidly growing data, implementing an efficient and effective data storage and retention strategy is crucial for organizations to maintain operational efficiency, reduce costs, ensure regulatory compliance, and protect sensitive information. By carefully considering storage options, retention policies, archiving needs, and data management best practices, organizations can optimize their data storage infrastructure while supporting their long-term business goals. Whether for network telemetry, application logs, or business intelligence data, a well-executed storage and retention strategy ensures that valuable data is preserved, accessible, and secure throughout its lifecycle.

Real-Time vs Historical Analysis Techniques

In network monitoring and performance analysis, understanding the distinction between real-time and historical analysis techniques is crucial for managing infrastructure effectively. Both techniques provide valuable insights, but they serve different purposes, require different approaches, and are often used together to provide a complete picture of a network's health, performance, and security. Real-time analysis focuses on the immediate state of a system, while historical analysis looks at trends and patterns over time. The integration of both techniques into a monitoring framework allows organizations to address immediate issues, track performance improvements, and make data-driven decisions for the future.

Real-time analysis refers to the continuous monitoring of network performance, providing instant feedback on the state of the system. It is designed to capture and process data as it happens, enabling immediate detection of issues such as bottlenecks, failures, or abnormal activity. In real-time analysis, the data is typically processed with minimal delay, often with near-instantaneous reporting to network administrators, operators, or automated systems. This allows for immediate corrective actions, whether manual or automated, to be taken. Real-time analysis is essential for mission-critical applications and systems where performance is directly tied to user experience, such as VoIP, financial transactions, cloud applications, and interactive services. For example, network latency spikes or packet loss can immediately degrade the quality of these services, and real-time monitoring helps to detect these issues promptly.

The advantage of real-time analysis is its ability to provide actionable insights in the moment, enabling network operators to address problems before they escalate. It supports proactive decision-making, ensuring that issues can be identified and corrected before they impact users or applications. Additionally, real-time analysis is crucial for security monitoring, as it enables the detection of suspicious behavior, such as DDoS attacks, unauthorized access, or anomalous traffic patterns, as soon as they occur. This capability to react immediately to network anomalies makes real-time monitoring an indispensable tool for maintaining the security and reliability of modern networks.

However, real-time analysis is not without its challenges. The primary limitation of real-time monitoring is its focus on the present moment, which means it often lacks the broader context needed to understand long-term trends. While it can provide immediate alerts and visibility into current network performance, it does not offer insight into the historical patterns that may have led to a particular issue. Additionally, real-time monitoring systems require significant resources to process large volumes of data in real time, particularly in high-traffic environments. These systems must be carefully tuned to balance the need for immediate feedback with the ability to scale to handle high throughput.

Historical analysis, on the other hand, focuses on collecting and analyzing data over extended periods to identify trends, patterns, and root causes of issues. This technique is invaluable for long-term performance assessment, troubleshooting, capacity planning, and strategic decision-making. By looking at historical data, organizations can identify recurring issues, track performance improvements or degradations, and understand how network usage evolves over time. Historical analysis typically involves the aggregation of large datasets, allowing operators to correlate various performance indicators and make informed predictions about future behavior. It is particularly effective in identifying underlying issues that may not be immediately apparent through real-time monitoring alone.

One of the primary benefits of historical analysis is its ability to provide context. While real-time analysis can alert operators to an issue, historical data allows for a deeper understanding of how that issue fits into long-term trends. For instance, historical bandwidth utilization data can help identify patterns of congestion that may have been caused by growing traffic demands over months or years. Similarly, historical analysis can reveal recurring spikes in network latency or packet loss during certain times of day or week, helping to identify issues that may be linked to scheduled maintenance, backup jobs, or traffic surges.

Historical analysis also plays a critical role in capacity planning and forecasting. By analyzing historical usage patterns, network teams can predict future growth and ensure that resources are available to meet upcoming demands. Historical data provides the insight needed to plan for infrastructure upgrades, whether scaling up hardware or optimizing network configurations. It allows organizations to make data-driven decisions about when to invest in additional capacity, which can help avoid overprovisioning or underutilization of resources.

The main challenge of historical analysis lies in the time and resources required to collect, store, and analyze large amounts of data. Unlike real-time monitoring, which focuses on processing data as it is generated, historical analysis requires storing vast quantities of information for extended periods. This can result in significant storage costs, especially when dealing with high-frequency telemetry or long-term retention requirements. Additionally, analyzing historical data can be computationally intensive, requiring advanced tools and techniques to process and extract meaningful insights. As the volume of data grows, organizations must ensure they have the right infrastructure in place to manage and analyze it effectively.

While real-time and historical analysis each have their unique strengths, they are often most effective when used together in a complementary manner. The combination of both approaches allows organizations to gain a comprehensive view of their network's health and performance, enabling both immediate responses and long-term strategic decisions. Real-time monitoring provides the immediate visibility and alerts needed to address issues as they arise, while historical analysis offers the deeper insights required to understand the root causes of problems, optimize performance over time, and plan for future growth.

For example, an organization might use real-time monitoring to detect a sudden spike in latency on a critical application. Once the issue is identified and addressed, historical analysis can be used to investigate the root cause of the problem by examining past performance data and identifying any recurring patterns. By correlating real-time data with historical trends, operators can pinpoint whether the latency spike was caused by an unexpected surge in traffic, a configuration issue, or a failure in the underlying infrastructure. This combined approach allows for both rapid response and continuous improvement.

Another advantage of integrating both real-time and historical analysis is the ability to support predictive analytics and machine learning. By combining real-time data with historical trends, machine learning algorithms can identify patterns that might not be immediately obvious. These systems can then predict potential issues before they occur, allowing for even greater proactive management of network health. For instance, predictive analytics could forecast when network congestion is likely to occur based on historical traffic patterns, enabling the network team to take preventative actions such as traffic rerouting or resource provisioning.

Real-time and historical analysis are two complementary techniques that form the backbone of modern network management and performance monitoring. While real-time analysis enables immediate action and responsive troubleshooting, historical analysis provides the broader context and deeper insights needed for long-term planning and optimization. By combining these techniques, organizations can achieve a more comprehensive understanding of their network, proactively address issues, and make data-driven decisions that enhance both performance and security.

Visualization Tools for Network Data

In modern network management, the ability to effectively visualize network data is a critical component for ensuring the performance, reliability, and security of an infrastructure. Network data is often complex, dynamic, and voluminous, requiring advanced visualization tools to present it in ways that are easy to interpret and act upon. These tools allow network administrators, engineers, and security teams to quickly identify issues, track performance metrics, and make data-driven decisions. By transforming raw data into actionable visual representations, visualization tools help users understand the health and state of their networks at a glance. Whether it is monitoring traffic flows, analyzing bandwidth usage, or diagnosing security incidents, the right visualization tool can significantly enhance an organization's ability to manage its network effectively.

Network monitoring systems generate vast amounts of data, and understanding this data is often the most challenging part of network management. Raw data in the form of logs, statistics, and telemetry can be overwhelming without proper tools to display it in a structured and understandable way. Visualization tools help bridge this gap by providing a graphical interface through which network performance and health can be monitored. These tools can display everything from real-time network traffic and system resource usage to historical trends and security events, all in a format that simplifies the analysis process. Without these visualization capabilities, network operators would be left sifting through raw data, making it difficult to gain insights or detect issues in a timely manner.

One of the key advantages of network data visualization is its ability to present complex data sets in a more digestible and user-friendly format. For example, a simple line chart may represent real-time bandwidth usage over a given period, while heatmaps can indicate the intensity of network traffic across different regions or devices. Pie charts or bar graphs can show the distribution of traffic types, such as HTTP, DNS, or FTP, giving network administrators an at-a-glance understanding of how resources are being consumed. These visualizations allow administrators to spot trends, anomalies, and potential issues more quickly than by analyzing raw data or numeric outputs alone. By providing an immediate visual representation of key metrics, visualization tools help teams make faster, more informed decisions.

Real-time visualization tools are particularly beneficial in fast-paced network environments, where quick responses are required to ensure the stability and performance of critical systems. Network performance monitoring tools often integrate with data visualization platforms to offer live monitoring dashboards that reflect current network conditions. These dashboards typically include graphical elements such as real-time graphs, gauges, and maps that update continuously, offering an up-to-date view of the network's health. For example, real-time visualizations can show bandwidth utilization, latency, packet loss, and system resource consumption as they happen, allowing operators to identify issues like congestion or device failures immediately. By visualizing this data in real time, network engineers can respond promptly to issues, avoiding costly downtimes and performance degradation.

Another critical aspect of visualization tools is their ability to handle large-scale, distributed network environments. In large organizations, networks are often spread across multiple locations, with numerous devices, servers, and endpoints connected across various geographical regions. A network visualization tool capable of integrating data from multiple sources is vital for providing a comprehensive overview of the entire network. These tools can present the status of each device, connection, and network segment on a single, unified dashboard. Network maps, for instance, provide a visual representation of the network topology, showing how different devices are connected and where potential points of failure or bottlenecks exist. This holistic view is essential for large enterprises with complex network infrastructures, as it allows administrators to pinpoint issues across a diverse and expansive environment.

Historical data visualization is equally important in network management. While real-time monitoring provides immediate visibility into network performance, historical data enables deeper insights into trends, patterns, and long-term performance. Visualization tools that allow for the display of historical data trends help organizations analyze past network behavior and make better-informed decisions about future planning and capacity expansion. For instance, network administrators can use historical data to track bandwidth usage over time, identify traffic spikes, and assess how traffic patterns change based on different conditions. This is especially valuable for capacity planning, where organizations can predict future network needs based on past usage trends and avoid over-provisioning or under-provisioning network resources.

The integration of machine learning and artificial intelligence into network visualization tools has further enhanced their effectiveness. These technologies can analyze vast amounts of network data to detect anomalies, identify potential security threats, and predict future performance issues. AI-powered visualization tools can highlight unusual patterns, such as unexpected surges in traffic or unusual communication between devices, and present these in easy-to-understand visual formats. By leveraging machine learning algorithms, these tools can provide deeper insights into network behavior, enabling network operators to identify problems that may otherwise go unnoticed. Additionally, predictive analytics can help network engineers plan for potential issues before they occur, optimizing network performance and ensuring stability.

Security visualization is another essential feature of modern network data visualization tools. With increasing cybersecurity threats, organizations need tools that can help identify and respond to security incidents in real time. Visualization tools for security provide a graphical representation of security events, such as unauthorized access attempts, malware activity, or DDoS attacks. These tools often integrate with Security Information and Event Management (SIEM) systems to offer a visual overview of security threats across the network. The ability to visualize security incidents on a map or graph allows security teams to prioritize and respond to threats more efficiently, reducing the time it takes to mitigate potential breaches.

While the benefits of network data visualization are clear, implementing effective visualization tools comes with its own set of challenges. One of the main challenges is ensuring that the right data is being captured and presented. Too much data can overwhelm the visualization, making it difficult for users to focus on the most important information. It is essential to filter out irrelevant data and present only the metrics that are most critical to network performance and security. Additionally, the complexity of the network itself can make it difficult to represent all the relevant information in a single, cohesive view. This often requires customization and configuration of the visualization tools to ensure that the data is presented in a meaningful way.

Another challenge lies in integrating data from different sources and systems. Network environments today are highly dynamic, with a variety of devices, services, and platforms generating data. To provide a comprehensive view of the network, visualization tools must be able to aggregate data from various sources, such as SNMP, NetFlow, telemetry, and other monitoring systems. Ensuring that these diverse data sets can be seamlessly integrated into a single visualization platform is crucial for maintaining an accurate and up-to-date picture of the network's health.

Visualization tools for network data are indispensable for modern network management, offering an intuitive way to monitor performance, track security events, and analyze network behavior. By providing graphical representations of complex data, these tools enable faster, more informed decision-making, helping administrators respond to issues quickly and efficiently. The integration of AI and machine learning further enhances their capabilities, enabling predictive insights and more effective problem detection. As networks continue to grow in complexity and scale, the role of visualization tools will only become more critical in ensuring the effective management and security of network infrastructures.

Anomaly Detection and Root Cause Analysis

Anomaly detection and root cause analysis are two of the most vital components of modern network monitoring, ensuring that performance issues, security threats, and other operational problems are quickly identified and effectively addressed. These techniques are essential for maintaining the health and reliability of network systems, particularly as networks grow more complex and dynamic. With the rise of distributed infrastructures, real-time telemetry data, and sophisticated threats, organizations must rely on advanced tools and methods to detect deviations from normal behavior and identify the underlying causes of issues. While anomaly detection helps identify unusual patterns that may signal problems, root cause analysis goes a step further by pinpointing the exact cause of these anomalies, enabling administrators to take informed corrective actions.

Anomaly detection is the process of identifying patterns in network traffic, system behavior, or application performance that deviate from what is considered normal. These deviations could indicate a variety of issues, ranging from network congestion and hardware failures to cyberattacks and misconfigurations. The primary goal of anomaly detection is to identify unusual events or conditions that could lead to performance degradation, security breaches, or service disruptions. To do this effectively, monitoring systems must first establish a baseline of normal network behavior. This baseline is typically derived from historical data, network traffic patterns, and performance metrics that reflect the typical operation of the network over time. Once this baseline is established, any significant deviation from it can be flagged as an anomaly.

The key challenge in anomaly detection is defining what constitutes "normal" behavior. With dynamic networks, constantly changing traffic patterns, and varying workloads, defining a single set of thresholds or patterns for normal behavior can be difficult. Traditional approaches often rely on simple threshold-based methods, where any metric exceeding a predefined limit (such as CPU usage or bandwidth utilization) triggers an alert. While this method can be effective in some cases, it can also lead to false positives, especially in high-traffic environments where short-term spikes are common and not necessarily indicative of a problem. More advanced techniques use statistical models, machine learning algorithms, or artificial intelligence to dynamically learn what normal behavior looks like and identify deviations without relying on static thresholds. These techniques continuously adapt to changes in network conditions, improving their accuracy over time and reducing the likelihood of false alarms.

Machine learning (ML) plays a particularly important role in modern anomaly detection. By training algorithms on historical data, these models can learn to identify subtle patterns in network traffic and behavior that may be difficult for traditional methods to detect. For example, machine learning models can recognize anomalies in traffic that might indicate a slow-building DDoS attack or unusual communication patterns between devices that could signify a breach or malware activity. These systems can be trained to detect both known threats, such as signature-based attacks, and unknown threats that may not fit predefined patterns. As these systems process more data, they become better at distinguishing between normal fluctuations and genuine threats, allowing for more accurate detection of anomalous events.

Once an anomaly is detected, the next step is root cause analysis, which focuses on identifying the underlying cause of the issue. While anomaly detection provides the initial alert that something is wrong, root cause analysis digs deeper to find out why the anomaly occurred in the first place. Effective root cause analysis involves collecting and correlating data from multiple sources across the network to trace the problem back to its origin. This could involve analyzing telemetry data, logs, configuration files, performance metrics, and even historical trends to understand how the anomaly developed and what triggered it.

The process of root cause analysis begins with data aggregation. Since network environments are composed of numerous interconnected devices, systems, and services, a problem could have multiple contributing factors. Collecting data from various sources allows analysts to build a comprehensive view of the issue. Telemetry data provides real-time performance metrics, such as bandwidth utilization, packet loss, and latency, while log files might reveal error messages or warnings that occurred around the same time as the anomaly. By combining these data sources, root cause analysis can identify correlations and patterns that might indicate the source of the problem.

One common approach to root cause analysis is using dependency mapping and topology analysis. In a large network, devices, services, and applications are often interconnected, with performance issues in one area having ripple effects throughout the entire system. By visualizing the network topology and understanding the dependencies between various components, analysts can quickly identify which devices or services are affected by the anomaly This can be particularly useful in identifying issues such as misconfigured network devices, overloaded servers, or failing hardware. For example, if an anomaly is detected in network traffic between two devices, a topology map can reveal if there are any intermediary devices, such as routers or switches, that might be contributing to the issue.

Automated root cause analysis tools often use artificial intelligence and machine learning to assist in the analysis process. These systems can automatically correlate data from different sources, detect patterns, and even suggest potential causes of the anomaly based on historical data and known issues. This reduces the time and effort required for manual analysis and helps identify the root cause faster. AI-driven systems can also continuously learn from past incidents, improving their ability to detect and analyze future problems.

Effective root cause analysis also involves collaboration between different teams. Network engineers, system administrators, security professionals, and application developers often need to work together to resolve complex issues that span multiple layers of the infrastructure. Root cause analysis tools that provide a unified view of the network and its components help facilitate this collaboration by allowing teams to access the same data and insights in real time. This ensures that the right stakeholders are involved in the problem-solving process and that the issue can be resolved quickly and efficiently.

The benefits of combining anomaly detection and root cause analysis extend beyond immediate troubleshooting. By regularly analyzing network performance and security incidents, organizations can identify trends and potential risks before they develop into larger problems. This proactive approach to network management helps prevent downtime, reduce the impact of security breaches, and ensure that resources are allocated efficiently. Furthermore, organizations can use insights gained from root cause analysis to improve network design, optimize configurations, and prevent similar issues from occurring in the future.

In summary, anomaly detection and root cause analysis are two complementary techniques that work together to ensure the reliability and security of modern networks. Anomaly detection helps identify when something goes wrong, while root cause analysis provides the tools and methods necessary to understand why it happened and how to fix it. By leveraging machine learning, real-time data collection, and advanced analytics, these techniques enable network teams to respond more quickly to issues, minimize downtime, and optimize network performance. The integration of both anomaly detection and root cause analysis into network management processes is essential for maintaining a stable, secure, and high-performing network environment.

Machine Learning in Network Monitoring

Machine learning has emerged as a transformative technology in the field of network monitoring, enabling organizations to gain deeper insights, improve performance, and enhance security through intelligent automation. Traditional network monitoring approaches, which rely on manual rule sets, thresholds, and basic anomaly detection techniques, have proven to be insufficient in the face of modern, dynamic, and increasingly complex networks. As networks grow in size and sophistication, managing them effectively requires more advanced tools that can not only detect problems but also predict and proactively address them. Machine learning (ML) provides a powerful solution to these challenges by analyzing vast amounts of network data, identifying patterns, and making data-driven predictions that help optimize network operations.

The application of machine learning in network monitoring primarily involves training models on historical data to detect anomalies, predict network behavior, and automate decision-making. One of the key advantages of machine learning in this context is its ability to learn from data without the need for explicit programming or rule-setting. Traditional monitoring systems often rely on predefined thresholds to trigger alerts or actions, but these systems can struggle to adapt to changes in network behavior or unexpected patterns. Machine learning, on the other hand, uses data to build models that can evolve over time, automatically adapting to new network conditions and identifying patterns that would be difficult or impossible to detect using manual methods.

A common use case for machine learning in network monitoring is anomaly detection. In a network environment, anomalies can manifest in many ways, such as unusual traffic patterns, spikes in bandwidth usage, or unexpected changes in application performance. Detecting these anomalies quickly is critical to maintaining network reliability and security. Machine learning models can be trained to recognize normal network behavior based on historical data, and any deviation from this behavior can be flagged as an anomaly. For example, a sudden surge in traffic on a previously unused network path could indicate a potential DDoS attack or a misconfigured device. ML algorithms are well-suited for identifying these types of issues in real time, enabling network operators to respond swiftly and prevent service disruptions or security breaches.

Machine learning is particularly effective at identifying subtle, complex patterns in data that may not be immediately obvious through traditional monitoring methods. For instance, network monitoring systems can use supervised learning techniques, where models are trained using labeled data to classify network events into categories such as normal, malicious, or suspicious. These models can then be applied to real-time data to continuously monitor the network, flagging potential issues as they arise. In the case of unsupervised learning, models can be used to detect outliers or clusters of unusual behavior without requiring predefined labels. This makes unsupervised learning especially valuable for identifying novel threats or unknown patterns, such as zero-day attacks or previously unseen network vulnerabilities.

Another critical area where machine learning can improve network monitoring is in performance optimization. ML algorithms can analyze data such as bandwidth usage, latency, packet loss, and system resource consumption to predict future network demand. By identifying trends and patterns in these performance metrics, machine learning can help network administrators optimize resource allocation, ensuring that the network is running efficiently and that potential bottlenecks are addressed before they affect users. For example, by analyzing historical bandwidth usage data, an ML model might predict peak traffic times and recommend proactive measures such as bandwidth throttling or rerouting traffic to less congested paths. This capability allows networks to be more adaptive and responsive, reducing the need for manual intervention and improving overall performance.

Machine learning also plays a crucial role in network security, where it can be used to identify and mitigate potential threats before they escalate. Traditional security monitoring systems often rely on signature-based methods, where known attack patterns or signatures are matched against network traffic. While this approach is effective for identifying known threats, it is limited in its ability to detect new, unknown attacks. Machine learning can enhance security monitoring by analyzing traffic patterns and identifying behaviors that deviate from normal activity, which may indicate the presence of a security threat. For example, machine learning models can be trained to detect patterns associated with DDoS attacks, data exfiltration, or lateral movement within the network. Once an anomaly is detected, the system can alert security teams, automate defensive actions, or even block malicious traffic in real time, reducing the impact of security incidents.

One of the significant advantages of using machine learning in network monitoring is its ability to scale. As networks grow in size and complexity, the volume of data generated by devices, applications, and network traffic becomes overwhelming. Traditional monitoring systems struggle to process and analyze this vast amount of data in real time, leading to delayed responses and missed threats. Machine learning, however, can handle large-scale data processing, analyzing millions of data points simultaneously and identifying trends and anomalies across the entire network. This scalability makes machine learning a powerful tool for managing modern, large-scale networks, where real-time decision-making and automated responses are critical for maintaining performance and security.

Another area where machine learning is transforming network monitoring is in predictive analytics. By leveraging historical data, machine learning models can forecast future network behavior, helping organizations plan for future capacity needs, optimize configurations, and avoid potential issues. For example, a machine learning model trained on historical traffic patterns can predict periods of high demand, allowing network administrators to proactively allocate resources or adjust configurations to ensure that the network can handle the increased load. This predictive capability is valuable for capacity planning, as it helps organizations anticipate network growth and avoid performance bottlenecks before they occur.

Despite its many advantages, implementing machine learning in network monitoring comes with its own set of challenges. One of the main challenges is the quality of the data used to train the models. Machine learning algorithms rely on large amounts of high-quality, labeled data to learn patterns and make accurate predictions. In many cases, network data may be noisy, incomplete, or unstructured, which can hinder the performance of machine learning models. Ensuring that the data used for training is clean, accurate, and representative of real-world network conditions is crucial for achieving reliable results.

Another challenge is the complexity of deploying and maintaining machine learning models in network monitoring systems. Developing and training machine learning models requires specialized expertise in data science and machine learning algorithms. Furthermore, models must be continuously updated and retrained to adapt to changing network conditions and emerging threats. As a result, organizations need skilled personnel and ongoing resources to ensure that their machine learning systems remain effective and up-to-date.

Machine learning is becoming an integral part of network monitoring, providing valuable insights into performance, security, and resource optimization. By enabling the automated detection of anomalies, predicting future network behavior, and improving security, machine learning helps organizations proactively manage their networks, reduce downtime, and enhance user experience. As the complexity of networks continues to grow, machine learning will play an increasingly critical role in ensuring that networks remain secure, efficient, and resilient. The ability to process large volumes of data, identify subtle patterns, and adapt to changing conditions makes machine learning an indispensable tool for modern network monitoring.

Cloud Network Monitoring with Modern Protocols

As businesses increasingly migrate their infrastructure to the cloud, the need for effective cloud network monitoring has become more critical than ever before. Cloud environments are dynamic, scalable, and often involve multi-cloud and hybrid architectures, which present unique challenges for network monitoring. Unlike traditional on-premises networks, cloud networks are typically decentralized, with resources distributed across various regions and services. This distributed nature requires new approaches to network monitoring that can handle the complexities of cloud-based infrastructure. Modern protocols play a pivotal role in providing visibility, ensuring performance, and maintaining security in cloud networks. By leveraging these protocols, organizations can gain deeper insights into their cloud infrastructure, enabling proactive management and rapid issue resolution.

Cloud network monitoring involves tracking the performance and health of the cloud resources that make up the infrastructure. This includes monitoring the performance of cloud instances, virtual networks, storage resources, and even cloud-native applications. Traditional monitoring systems often rely on SNMP or other polling-based protocols, but these are not always well-suited to cloud environments. Cloud providers like Amazon Web Services (AWS), Microsoft Azure, and Google Cloud offer native monitoring tools, but these tools are often limited to the specific services within the provider's ecosystem. To achieve a comprehensive view of a multi-cloud or hybrid cloud environment, organizations must use modern monitoring protocols that can integrate data from various sources and deliver actionable insights in real time.

Modern protocols such as gNMI, gRPC, and OpenTelemetry are well-suited for cloud network monitoring. These protocols are designed to provide high-resolution, low-latency data in real-time, which is crucial for monitoring the fast-paced, elastic nature of cloud networks. gNMI (gRPC Network Management Interface), in particular, offers a standardized way of interacting with cloud-based networking devices, enabling continuous telemetry data streams. gNMI is often used in combination with YANG data models, which provide a structured representation of the data being monitored, making it easier to collect, analyze, and respond to network changes.

gRPC, the transport protocol used by gNMI, is another modern solution that has found a place in cloud network monitoring. gRPC allows for efficient, high-performance communication between services across different cloud environments. It is based on HTTP/2 and supports features such as multiplexing and bidirectional streaming, making it ideal for transmitting large volumes of telemetry data in real-time. The ability to send and receive data continuously, without the overhead of traditional request-response protocols, makes gRPC highly effective for cloud network monitoring, where real-time data is essential for ensuring performance and security.

Another protocol gaining traction in cloud network monitoring is OpenTelemetry, an open-source framework that provides a set of APIs, libraries, agents, and instrumentation for collecting distributed traces and metrics from cloud-based applications and services. OpenTelemetry supports a wide variety of cloud platforms and technologies, making it an excellent choice for organizations with multi-cloud or hybrid cloud infrastructures. By standardizing the way monitoring data is collected, OpenTelemetry allows for seamless integration with a range of monitoring tools and analytics platforms, enabling organizations to gain a unified view of their cloud network's performance. OpenTelemetry can be used to monitor not only network traffic but also application-level performance, such as response times, error rates, and throughput, offering a more comprehensive approach to cloud monitoring.

The advantage of using modern protocols like gNMI, gRPC, and OpenTelemetry lies in their ability to provide granular, real-time telemetry data. In cloud environments, where applications and services are continuously scaled up or down based on demand, it is crucial to monitor network performance on a per-instance or per-service level. Traditional monitoring tools often lack the capability to handle this level of granularity, resulting in blind spots and delays in identifying issues. Modern protocols overcome this limitation by enabling continuous data streams from cloud-based resources, allowing administrators to monitor and respond to network events in real time.

In addition to providing real-time monitoring, modern protocols offer greater flexibility in how monitoring data is collected and analyzed. Unlike traditional SNMP-based systems, which rely on periodic polling, gNMI and OpenTelemetry support event-driven architectures that push data to collectors only when significant changes occur. This reduces the load on both the monitoring system and the network, ensuring that resources are used efficiently. Furthermore, because these protocols are designed to work across different cloud platforms, they enable the collection of data from various sources in a unified manner, eliminating the need for siloed monitoring systems.

Cloud network monitoring also benefits from the integration of machine learning (ML) and artificial intelligence (AI) capabilities. By using modern protocols to collect vast amounts of telemetry data, organizations can apply ML algorithms to analyze this data and identify patterns, predict future performance trends, and detect anomalies. For example, ML models can predict traffic spikes, helping organizations to proactively adjust resources before bottlenecks occur. AI-based anomaly detection can identify unusual patterns in network traffic, alerting administrators to potential security threats such as DDoS attacks or unauthorized access attempts. The integration of ML and AI with cloud network monitoring provides a more intelligent, automated approach to network management, reducing the need for manual intervention and improving response times.

One of the challenges of cloud network monitoring is the inherent complexity of cloud architectures, which are often made up of numerous interconnected services and dynamic components. Traditional monitoring tools that rely on static configurations or manual inputs may struggle to keep up with the fast-paced changes in cloud environments. Modern protocols like gNMI and OpenTelemetry, however, are built to handle dynamic, elastic environments. These protocols allow administrators to monitor both static and dynamic components of the network, adapting to changes in the infrastructure in real time. Whether a new virtual machine is provisioned or a container is scaled down, these protocols can capture the necessary telemetry data to ensure the network is operating smoothly.

Security is another crucial consideration in cloud network monitoring. Cloud environments are often targeted by cybercriminals due to their openness and complexity. Modern monitoring protocols enable more effective detection of security incidents by providing real-time visibility into network traffic, authentication logs, and system activity. For example, gNMI and OpenTelemetry can track the flow of data across virtual networks, enabling organizations to detect unauthorized access, unusual traffic patterns, or configuration changes that could indicate a breach. With continuous monitoring, potential security threats can be identified before they escalate, helping to prevent data breaches and other security incidents.

Cloud network monitoring with modern protocols is essential for organizations that rely on cloud infrastructure to deliver services. By leveraging protocols like gNMI, gRPC, and OpenTelemetry, businesses can gain the visibility, scalability, and flexibility needed to effectively manage their cloud networks. These protocols enable real-time data collection, integration across multiple cloud environments, and enhanced security, all while reducing the overhead associated with traditional monitoring tools. With the ability to collect granular, actionable data in real time, organizations can optimize performance, ensure security, and deliver a better experience for users. As cloud computing continues to evolve, modern monitoring protocols will play an increasingly critical role in maintaining the health, performance, and security of cloud networks.

Monitoring SDN and Virtualized Environments

As the demand for more flexible, scalable, and efficient networks increases, many organizations are turning to Software-Defined Networking (SDN) and virtualization to meet these needs. SDN and virtualized environments enable centralized control and the abstraction of network resources, allowing for dynamic configuration, resource allocation, and improved agility. However, the complexity and dynamic nature of SDN and virtualized environments present new challenges for network monitoring. Traditional network monitoring tools, which were designed for static, hardware-based networks, often struggle to provide adequate visibility and control over these highly flexible, virtualized networks. Monitoring SDN and virtualized environments requires new tools and approaches that can handle the complexities of these dynamic, software-driven networks.

In an SDN architecture, the control plane is decoupled from the data plane, meaning that the decision-making process about where traffic should go is separated from the actual forwarding of packets. The controller is central to the network's operation, making decisions about routing, load balancing, and traffic engineering. Unlike traditional networks where these decisions are distributed across network devices, SDN centralizes the intelligence of the network in the controller. This centralization offers significant advantages in terms of flexibility, scalability, and automation, but it also means that monitoring must focus not just on the individual devices but on the controller's behavior and how it interacts with the network infrastructure. Monitoring SDN environments requires real-time data on controller performance, the health of virtualized network devices, and the status of data flows across the entire network. It also requires an understanding of how policies are applied and whether they are being enforced effectively across all network components.

One of the key challenges in monitoring SDN is maintaining visibility into the network's dynamic state. SDN networks are highly flexible, with network resources often reallocated, resized, or even reprogrammed on the fly. This creates an ever-changing network landscape that is difficult to capture using traditional monitoring tools. To address this, SDN monitoring tools need to integrate tightly with the SDN controller and collect real-time data on traffic patterns, link utilization, and device health. The controller itself can provide telemetry data that gives administrators insight into the state of the network, such as network topology changes, flow modifications, and resource usage. By integrating monitoring systems directly into the SDN controller, operators can obtain comprehensive views of the entire network and make more informed decisions about performance optimization and troubleshooting.

In virtualized environments, the challenges of monitoring are similarly complex. Virtualization abstracts physical hardware and enables multiple virtual machines (VMs) or containers to share the same physical resources. While this offers improved resource utilization and agility, it also creates the challenge of monitoring virtual network traffic, performance metrics, and application behavior in an environment where physical boundaries are less clear. Virtualized environments often involve a mix of hypervisors, virtual switches, and virtual routers that interact with physical hardware, and traditional monitoring tools are not equipped to provide the level of visibility required in these environments. Effective monitoring of virtualized environments must track the performance of not only the virtual machines but also the virtual network functions (VNFs) and the underlying infrastructure supporting them.

To monitor virtualized environments, administrators rely on specialized tools that can track both the virtualized and physical components of the network. Virtualization monitoring tools provide insight into the performance of VMs, containers, and hypervisors, as well as the network traffic between virtual machines and across physical links. In addition to resource usage data, these tools must be able to collect metrics on virtual network traffic, such as packet loss, latency, and throughput, and correlate this data with physical network performance. Monitoring tools that are designed for virtualized environments often integrate with SDN controllers to provide a more holistic view of the network's performance, enabling administrators to correlate virtual machine metrics with SDN-based network traffic flows.

One of the critical aspects of monitoring SDN and virtualized environments is ensuring the health and performance of the underlying network infrastructure. While SDN provides flexibility in how data is forwarded and routed, the network infrastructure still relies on physical hardware, such as switches, routers, and links, to transport data. Monitoring the physical components is just as important as monitoring the virtualized components, especially in SDN environments where network performance is influenced by both hardware and software. Monitoring solutions must collect data on the status of physical devices, such as CPU and memory usage, link performance, and hardware failures, while also monitoring the software-defined aspects of the network, such as flow paths and traffic policies.

Another significant challenge in SDN and virtualized environments is security monitoring. The flexibility and programmability of SDN can create new opportunities for network attacks, such as DDoS attacks, unauthorized access, or the manipulation of network flows. In virtualized environments, security issues can arise from misconfigurations, such as improper isolation between virtual machines or containers, which can lead to data leakage or unauthorized access. Security monitoring in SDN and virtualized environments requires specialized tools that can detect threats in both the virtual and physical layers of the network. This includes monitoring for anomalies in network traffic patterns, unauthorized changes to flow tables, and irregular behavior in virtualized applications. SDN and virtualization-based security solutions can provide greater visibility into security events, allowing for faster detection and response to potential threats.

Effective monitoring in SDN and virtualized environments also requires advanced analytics and automation. The sheer volume of data generated by SDN controllers, virtual machines, and network devices makes manual monitoring difficult. To address this, SDN monitoring tools often incorporate machine learning and artificial intelligence (AI) techniques that can analyze network behavior, detect patterns, and predict future issues. For example, AI-based monitoring systems can predict traffic spikes, identify resource constraints, and automatically adjust network configurations to optimize performance. Automation also plays a critical role in network management, as it allows for the dynamic adjustment of resources in response to real-time data, such as reallocating virtual machines or modifying network paths to reduce congestion.

One of the most significant advantages of SDN and virtualized network monitoring is the ability to automate responses to network events. In traditional networks, administrators often had to manually adjust configurations or troubleshoot issues based on performance data. In SDN and virtualized environments, the centralized control plane allows for automated policy enforcement and network adjustments in response to changing conditions. For example, if a particular segment of the network is experiencing high traffic, the SDN controller can automatically reroute traffic to avoid congestion. Similarly, if a virtual machine is underperforming, the monitoring system can trigger an automated scaling action to allocate additional resources. This level of automation increases operational efficiency and reduces the likelihood of human error in network management.

In monitoring SDN and virtualized environments, data collection, integration, and analysis are essential for ensuring that the network operates efficiently, securely, and without interruption. SDN controllers, virtualization platforms, and monitoring tools must work together to provide real-time insights into network performance, application behavior, and security threats. By leveraging advanced monitoring techniques and integrating with SDN controllers, organizations can gain the visibility they need to manage and optimize their networks, ensuring that they can meet the demands of modern business environments. As SDN and virtualization technologies continue to evolve, the monitoring tools and strategies used to support them will continue to advance, providing even more powerful solutions for managing the complexity and scale of today's networks.

Role of APIs in Modern Network Monitoring

In the modern world of network monitoring, the role of Application Programming Interfaces (APIs) has become increasingly crucial. As networks grow in complexity and organizations demand more dynamic, scalable, and flexible solutions, APIs offer a powerful way to integrate different monitoring systems, automate tasks, and provide a seamless flow of data across various platforms. APIs enable the interaction between diverse network components, providing real-time data that is essential for efficient network management and performance optimization. Their role in modern network monitoring extends beyond simple data retrieval, offering opportunities for deeper integration, enhanced automation, and better overall network performance.

The primary function of APIs in network monitoring is to provide a standardized way for different systems to communicate with each other. In traditional network management environments, various devices and monitoring tools often operated in isolation, making it difficult to integrate data from multiple sources or automate responses to network events. APIs address this challenge by enabling communication between devices, software systems, and external platforms. For example, a network monitoring tool can use APIs to retrieve performance metrics from routers, switches, firewalls, and other devices. Similarly, APIs allow network monitoring systems to push data to cloud services, analytics platforms, or alerting systems, creating an interconnected network monitoring ecosystem. This interoperability is essential for providing a comprehensive view of network performance and health.

As businesses move to more distributed environments, particularly with the rise of cloud and hybrid infrastructures, network monitoring tools must be able to scale and adapt to rapidly changing environments. APIs allow for this level of scalability by enabling monitoring systems to dynamically interact with new devices, applications, and services as they are deployed. When a new device or service is added to the network, APIs can automatically integrate it into the monitoring system, ensuring that it is included in real-time monitoring and data collection. This flexibility is vital in modern, fast-moving network environments where changes happen frequently, and static configurations can quickly become obsolete.

Moreover, APIs have significantly improved the automation capabilities of network monitoring. Manual interventions are often required in traditional monitoring systems to respond to changes in the network, troubleshoot issues, or configure devices. With the integration of APIs, these tasks can be automated, reducing human error, improving efficiency, and enabling faster responses to network events. For instance, when an anomaly or performance issue is detected, an API can trigger an automated workflow to reconfigure the network, reroute traffic, or even provision additional resources to resolve the issue without manual intervention. This level of automation not only improves network performance but also reduces the operational burden on network administrators, freeing them to focus on higher-level tasks.

In addition to automation, APIs play a key role in enhancing network visibility and analytics. Network monitoring solutions can leverage APIs to aggregate data from multiple sources, such as devices, applications, security platforms, and cloud services, into a single centralized dashboard. This centralized view is essential for network operators to understand how their network is performing and to identify areas for improvement. APIs also allow for advanced analytics and machine learning integration, providing deeper insights into network traffic patterns, resource utilization, and potential security threats. By pulling in data from various systems, APIs enable monitoring platforms to perform more sophisticated analyses, such as trend forecasting, anomaly detection, and predictive maintenance, which help organizations stay ahead of potential issues and optimize their network operations.

Another significant advantage of APIs in network monitoring is their ability to enhance security. In modern network environments, security is paramount, and APIs play a central role in providing the necessary data to monitor and secure the network. Network monitoring tools can use APIs to pull real-time data on security events, such as unauthorized access attempts, malware activity, or suspicious traffic patterns. This data can be used to trigger automated security responses, such as isolating compromised devices, blocking malicious traffic, or alerting security teams to take further action. Additionally, APIs can be used to integrate monitoring systems with Security Information and Event Management (SIEM) tools, providing a unified platform for monitoring both performance and security. By enabling better integration and real-time security monitoring, APIs help organizations maintain a more secure and resilient network.

Furthermore, APIs facilitate the integration of network monitoring systems with other enterprise IT systems, such as orchestration platforms, configuration management tools, and helpdesk systems. This integration is essential for creating an end-to-end automation workflow that spans across the entire IT environment. For example, when a performance issue is detected, an API can automatically create a helpdesk ticket, notify the appropriate support team, and trigger a series of diagnostic actions to resolve the issue. This level of integration helps streamline operations, improves response times, and ensures that issues are addressed promptly and efficiently. It also helps to break down silos between different teams, allowing for a more collaborative approach to network management and problem-solving.

The use of APIs in modern network monitoring also supports the development of custom monitoring solutions tailored to an organization's specific needs. Rather than relying on off-the-shelf solutions, organizations can use APIs to build customized monitoring platforms that are specifically designed to meet their unique requirements. APIs enable organizations to select the precise data they need to collect and analyze, integrate with third-party tools, and create bespoke workflows and alerts. This level of customization provides greater flexibility, allowing organizations to adapt their monitoring systems to their evolving needs, whether they are managing on-premises infrastructure, hybrid clouds, or multi-cloud environments.

The open-source movement has further enhanced the role of APIs in network monitoring. Many modern monitoring tools, such as Prometheus, Grafana, and OpenTelemetry, provide open APIs that allow organizations to extend their functionality, integrate with other systems, and contribute to the development of the tools themselves. This openness not only promotes innovation but also ensures that monitoring solutions remain adaptable and can evolve alongside changing network technologies and business requirements.

APIs also improve the overall user experience by enabling the creation of intuitive dashboards and interfaces that aggregate and visualize network data from multiple sources. Rather than having to manually query different devices or systems for performance data, administrators can use APIs to pull this data into user-friendly dashboards that present key metrics in an easily digestible format. These dashboards can be customized to show the most relevant data for a particular user or team, ensuring that the right information is always at hand. The ability to interact with monitoring systems via APIs also allows for the development of custom reporting and alerting features, further enhancing the monitoring capabilities of the network.

APIs have become indispensable in modern network monitoring, enabling greater automation, scalability, and flexibility. By providing a standardized way for different systems to communicate, APIs make it possible to integrate diverse monitoring tools, collect real-time data from a wide range of sources, and automate responses to network events. They enable advanced analytics, enhance network security, and facilitate the development of custom solutions that meet specific organizational needs. As networks continue to grow more complex and distributed, APIs will play an increasingly important role in ensuring that organizations can monitor and manage their networks effectively and efficiently.

Compliance and Auditing Through Monitoring

In the digital age, network compliance and auditing have become crucial for organizations of all sizes. With increasing regulatory requirements, the rapid evolution of security threats, and the growing complexity of network environments, organizations must implement robust monitoring systems to ensure they comply with industry standards, governmental regulations, and internal policies. Monitoring plays a vital role in both compliance and auditing by providing real-time visibility into network activities, enabling organizations to detect deviations, enforce policies, and maintain transparency for auditing purposes. The integration of monitoring solutions with compliance frameworks ensures that organizations can maintain operational integrity, demonstrate accountability, and minimize the risk of penalties or breaches.

Compliance monitoring involves continuously assessing and ensuring that network activities align with regulatory requirements such as the General Data Protection Regulation (GDPR), Health Insurance Portability and Accountability Act (HIPAA), Payment Card Industry Data Security Standard (PCI DSS), and others. These regulations often impose strict guidelines on data privacy, security controls, access management, and audit trails. In many cases, organizations are required to demonstrate how they are meeting these requirements and must provide verifiable evidence in the event of an audit. Network monitoring systems are essential tools in this process, as they provide the necessary visibility into network traffic, configurations, and access controls that are critical for proving compliance.

For example, in industries like finance or healthcare, compliance mandates often require encryption of sensitive data during transmission and storage. A monitoring system can track the use of encryption protocols across the network, generating reports that demonstrate compliance with these requirements. Similarly, regulations often require network access controls to ensure that only authorized users can access sensitive systems. Monitoring tools can continuously assess user authentication methods, log access attempts, and verify whether security policies are being followed. By collecting and analyzing this data in real time, organizations can ensure that security policies are being enforced and that unauthorized access attempts are promptly flagged and addressed.

Auditing is another area where network monitoring plays an essential role. Auditing involves reviewing and analyzing network activities, configurations, and security practices to verify that they align with organizational policies and compliance standards. Network monitoring systems are a key enabler of this process, as they capture and store detailed records of network events, including configuration changes, security incidents, and user activity. This data serves as the foundation for audit trails that can be reviewed during internal audits, external audits, or regulatory assessments. Having access to accurate and up-to-date auditing information is vital for proving compliance and demonstrating accountability to auditors, regulators, and stakeholders.

One of the key features of network monitoring tools in the context of auditing is their ability to generate logs that detail all network interactions. These logs can include information about who accessed what data, when, and from where. This level of granularity is crucial for ensuring that network activity is transparent and traceable. In the event of an audit or security breach, these logs provide the evidence needed to understand what happened and why. Logs can also help identify trends or patterns that might indicate non-compliant behavior, enabling organizations to address potential issues before they lead to more significant problems.

Monitoring tools also support the ongoing validation of security controls and network configurations. Many compliance regulations require organizations to demonstrate that their security measures are regularly tested and verified. Automated monitoring solutions can continuously evaluate network devices, applications, and systems to ensure they meet the required security standards. For instance, a monitoring system might check whether all devices are running the latest security patches, whether firewalls and intrusion detection systems are functioning correctly, or whether antivirus software is active. By automating these tasks, organizations can ensure that their security controls remain effective and compliant without requiring manual intervention.

In addition to detecting potential security risks, network monitoring systems can help organizations proactively manage compliance by continuously checking that configurations align with industry best practices and regulatory requirements. Misconfigurations are a common cause of non-compliance, as they can inadvertently expose sensitive data or provide unauthorized access. Network monitoring systems can flag configuration discrepancies in real time, allowing administrators to address issues quickly and avoid penalties. For example, monitoring tools can alert administrators if a network device is configured to allow unnecessary access to sensitive information, enabling corrective actions to be taken before any potential security breach or compliance violation occurs.

Furthermore, real-time monitoring of network traffic enables the identification of suspicious activities that may indicate a security threat or compliance violation. For instance, unusual traffic patterns, such as large data transfers or irregular access to sensitive data, may be indicative of a potential data breach or insider threat. Monitoring systems equipped with anomaly detection capabilities can flag these irregularities as soon as they occur, triggering alerts for investigation. This proactive approach helps organizations stay ahead of security threats and ensures they remain in compliance with regulatory requirements that mandate the protection of sensitive information.

Data retention is another critical aspect of compliance and auditing. Regulatory frameworks often require organizations to retain logs and monitoring data for extended periods, sometimes several years, for auditing purposes. Effective monitoring solutions include secure data storage and retention capabilities, allowing organizations to store and manage this data efficiently. By ensuring that logs and monitoring data are securely archived and easily accessible, organizations can demonstrate compliance with data retention requirements and provide auditors with the necessary records. These retention systems must also ensure that data is stored in a manner that complies with data privacy regulations, such as ensuring that personal data is anonymized or encrypted when necessary.

Network monitoring tools also enable the creation of customized reports that can be tailored to specific compliance or audit requirements. These reports can summarize key network events, highlight compliance violations, and provide insights into the effectiveness of security controls. By automating the report generation process, organizations can save time and effort while ensuring that audit trails are complete and accurate. Customizable reporting also ensures that organizations can present the most relevant information to auditors, regulators, or internal stakeholders, making the audit process more efficient and transparent.

The role of APIs in modern network monitoring further enhances compliance and auditing processes. APIs allow monitoring tools to integrate with other systems, such as Security Information and Event Management (SIEM) platforms, ticketing systems, and compliance management tools. By integrating these systems, organizations can automate the flow of compliance-related data, streamline the auditing process, and enhance their ability to respond to incidents. APIs also enable monitoring systems to provide data to external compliance frameworks, ensuring that regulatory requirements are continuously met and that any potential violations are detected and addressed.

In the context of compliance and auditing, network monitoring is not just about tracking data for the sake of monitoring; it is about creating a structured, proactive approach to ensuring that network activities meet the required standards. By implementing effective monitoring solutions, organizations can stay compliant with regulatory requirements, minimize risks, and build trust with clients, partners, and regulators. Through continuous monitoring, real-time alerts, and detailed auditing capabilities, network monitoring systems help organizations maintain a secure and compliant network environment while ensuring that they can demonstrate accountability when needed.

Future Trends in Network Monitoring Protocols

The field of network monitoring is undergoing significant transformations as technologies evolve and new challenges emerge. Traditional monitoring protocols, such as SNMP and NetFlow, have served as the foundation for network management for many years, but with the rise of cloud computing, Software-Defined Networking (SDN), virtualization, and the increasing complexity of network infrastructures, these older protocols are becoming less sufficient in meeting the demands of modern networks. As organizations continue to adopt more dynamic, distributed, and virtualized environments, there is an increasing need for more adaptive, real-time, and comprehensive monitoring protocols that can keep up with these changes. In this context, future trends in network monitoring protocols are focusing on greater scalability, flexibility, automation, and security.

One of the most prominent trends in network monitoring protocols is the move toward more real-time, continuous data streaming. Traditional protocols like SNMP rely on periodic polling, where network devices are queried at regular intervals for status updates. While this approach is simple and has worked for many years, it has its limitations in environments where rapid response times and continuous monitoring are critical. Real-time monitoring allows for more immediate insights into network conditions, enabling faster identification of performance issues, security threats, and anomalies. Modern protocols, such as gNMI and OpenTelemetry, are designed to provide continuous telemetry data, which helps administrators keep a constant watch on network activities without delays or gaps in data. These protocols use streaming models to deliver up-to-date information, enabling more proactive network management and faster responses to issues before they escalate.

Another emerging trend is the increasing use of machine learning and artificial intelligence (AI) in network monitoring protocols. Machine learning models can be applied to large volumes of network data to detect patterns, predict future behavior, and identify anomalies that may indicate security threats or performance bottlenecks. By integrating AI with monitoring protocols, organizations can achieve more sophisticated anomaly detection, capacity planning, and predictive maintenance. For example, AI-driven network monitoring systems could analyze historical traffic data and predict when a network segment is likely to experience congestion, allowing administrators to take preventive action. Similarly, AI can identify unusual network traffic patterns indicative of a security breach or an emerging DDoS attack, alerting security teams in real time. The integration of AI into network monitoring not only enhances detection capabilities but also automates decision-making processes, reducing the need for manual intervention and enabling more efficient network operations.

The evolution of cloud computing is also shaping the future of network monitoring protocols. As businesses migrate to hybrid and multi-cloud environments, monitoring tools must adapt to provide visibility across a wider range of platforms. Traditional network monitoring protocols often focus on physical devices and on-premises infrastructures, but cloud environments require a different approach. The complexity of cloud-native applications, dynamic resource allocation, and multi-tenant environments necessitate monitoring protocols that can capture data from diverse cloud services, virtual networks, and distributed applications. Future protocols will likely be designed with cloud integration in mind, enabling seamless monitoring across different cloud providers and on-premises systems. Open standards, such as OpenTelemetry, are already playing a key role in providing a unified way to collect and analyze data across cloud and on-prem environments, ensuring that network monitoring remains consistent regardless of the infrastructure being used.

Security is another critical area where future network monitoring protocols will evolve. With the growing sophistication of cyberattacks and the increasing reliance on interconnected systems, securing network monitoring systems themselves has become a top priority. The protocols used for monitoring must be designed to be resistant to security threats, ensuring the integrity and confidentiality of network data. Future network monitoring protocols will likely include more robust encryption, authentication, and access control features to protect monitoring data from being intercepted or tampered with. Additionally, protocols will need to adapt to support security features such as zero-trust architectures, where the network assumes that every device, user, and application could be a potential threat and verifies their trustworthiness continuously. Security-centric protocols will be integrated into monitoring solutions to detect and mitigate threats in real time, ensuring that monitoring systems themselves remain secure.

One trend that is gaining traction is the integration of network monitoring protocols with automation and orchestration platforms. The rapid expansion of network infrastructure, combined with the increasing complexity of networks, makes it difficult for administrators to manually manage and optimize network resources. Automation tools allow for the dynamic adjustment of network configurations based on real-time data provided by monitoring protocols. For example, if a monitoring system detects high latency or congestion in a specific part of the network, an automation system can automatically reroute traffic or scale resources to alleviate the issue. Similarly, network policies can be adjusted in real time based on monitoring data, ensuring that the network operates optimally without requiring manual intervention. By integrating monitoring protocols with automation and orchestration platforms, organizations can achieve more efficient, self-healing networks that can adapt to changing conditions automatically.

Furthermore, the growing adoption of edge computing is influencing the design of future network monitoring protocols. As more devices and applications are deployed at the edge of the network, there is an increasing need for localized monitoring capabilities. Edge computing involves processing data closer to the source of data generation, such as IoT devices, to reduce latency and improve performance. Future monitoring protocols will need to support edge environments by providing data collection, analysis, and decision-making capabilities at the edge. This will reduce the reliance on central monitoring systems and allow for quicker responses to local issues. Edge monitoring will also require lightweight protocols that can function efficiently in resource-constrained environments, ensuring that even small devices can participate in network monitoring and contribute to overall network visibility.

Interoperability between different monitoring systems and protocols is another critical trend shaping the future of network monitoring. As networks become more complex and heterogeneous, organizations are often using a mix of different tools, protocols, and platforms to manage their infrastructure. Future monitoring protocols will need to be designed with interoperability in mind, ensuring that they can communicate seamlessly with other tools and technologies. This could involve standardizing data formats, developing common interfaces, and creating open-source frameworks that enable different monitoring systems to share data and insights. The ability to integrate data from various sources, including SDN controllers, virtualized environments, cloud platforms, and physical devices, will be essential for providing a unified view of network health.

In the near future, we can expect to see the development of more adaptive, intelligent, and secure network monitoring protocols that cater to the needs of dynamic and evolving network infrastructures. These protocols will provide real-time insights, enhance automation, and support advanced security features, all while integrating seamlessly with cloud environments, edge computing, and other emerging technologies. With the increasing complexity and scale of modern networks, the future of network monitoring will rely on innovative protocols that not only capture and analyze data but also enable automated, intelligent decision-making, ensuring that networks remain secure, resilient, and efficient.

Case Studies from Service Providers and Enterprises

In the world of network management, both service providers and enterprises face similar challenges when it comes to maintaining the performance, security, and reliability of their networks. However, the scale, complexity, and specific demands of their environments can vary significantly. Service providers are typically responsible for delivering connectivity and services to a large number of customers, often across vast geographical areas, whereas enterprises focus on maintaining a secure and efficient network within their own organization, often with a greater emphasis on internal applications and user experience. Both types of organizations, however, have embraced advanced monitoring and management techniques, leveraging various tools and strategies to overcome the unique challenges they face. Through these case studies, we can gain valuable insights into how network monitoring systems have been deployed and optimized to meet these challenges.

A key example can be seen in the approach of a large telecommunications service provider that serves millions of customers across multiple regions. This provider was facing significant issues related to network congestion, customer churn, and service outages, which were affecting customer satisfaction and their ability to deliver consistent service quality. In the past, the company relied on traditional monitoring systems that were limited in scope, mostly based on SNMP polling and threshold-based alerts. However, these methods proved ineffective in a network environment that was becoming more dynamic due to the introduction of SDN, cloud technologies, and the increasing demand for real-time services such as VoIP and streaming.

To address these challenges, the service provider implemented a comprehensive network monitoring solution that integrated real-time telemetry data, machine learning models, and predictive analytics. By adopting a modern protocol like gNMI (gRPC Network Management Interface) to collect telemetry data from network devices, the provider was able to move away from polling and gain continuous insights into network performance. This allowed the provider to detect issues such as congestion, latency, and packet loss in real time, before they impacted customers. Additionally, machine learning algorithms were employed to analyze historical data and predict future traffic patterns, allowing the provider to proactively allocate resources and prevent network congestion during peak usage times.

This shift in approach had significant positive impacts on both operational efficiency and customer experience. The real-time monitoring system allowed the service provider to detect and resolve issues more quickly, reducing downtime and improving overall service availability. The predictive analytics capabilities helped to optimize network resources and improve network planning, ensuring that the provider could scale its infrastructure to meet future demands. The integration of machine learning also enhanced the provider's ability to detect anomalies that were not immediately apparent through traditional methods, enabling faster identification of potential security threats or network misconfigurations.

On the enterprise side, a large multinational corporation with operations across several continents was struggling to manage the performance and security of its network infrastructure. The company relied heavily on cloud-based applications and services, as well as a hybrid cloud environment that connected its on-premises data centers to public cloud platforms. With an increasingly remote workforce and a growing reliance on cloud resources, the enterprise faced challenges in ensuring consistent performance, security, and compliance across its network. Existing monitoring tools, which were mainly focused on traditional network infrastructures, were ill-equipped to handle the complexities of cloud-native applications and virtualized resources.

To address these challenges, the enterprise deployed a comprehensive monitoring solution that integrated OpenTelemetry and cloud-native monitoring tools with its existing network monitoring infrastructure.

OpenTelemetry was used to collect distributed tracing and metrics from applications running across different cloud platforms and data centers. By collecting data at both the infrastructure and application levels, the company gained end-to-end visibility into its network, enabling better performance optimization and faster issue detection. The integration of monitoring tools for both on-premises and cloud environments ensured that the enterprise could maintain visibility across its entire network, regardless of whether resources were deployed in the public cloud or within its own data centers.

One of the significant outcomes of this approach was the ability to improve application performance. By monitoring cloud service interactions and infrastructure dependencies in real time, the enterprise could identify performance bottlenecks or resource constraints that were impacting user experience. For example, the monitoring system revealed that certain cloud services were experiencing delays due to resource contention, particularly during high-traffic periods. By addressing these issues proactively, the enterprise was able to reduce downtime and optimize the performance of critical applications, such as those supporting customer-facing services.

Moreover, security monitoring was enhanced through the integration of monitoring tools with the enterprise's security information and event management (SIEM) system. This integration enabled the real-time monitoring of network traffic, application behavior, and user activity across both the internal network and cloud environments. Anomalous activities, such as unexpected access patterns or unusual traffic from remote employees, were flagged and investigated promptly. This improved the enterprise's ability to detect and respond to security incidents more quickly, minimizing the risk of breaches or data leaks.

Another significant case study comes from a global e-commerce company that faced constant challenges in managing its network performance during peak shopping seasons. The company's infrastructure included a mixture of on-premises data centers and cloud-based services, and it needed a robust monitoring solution to ensure that its network could handle spikes in traffic during events like Black Friday or Cyber Monday. Traditional monitoring tools were not sufficient for predicting the sudden surges in traffic and ensuring that the network remained responsive during these high-demand periods.

To solve this problem, the e-commerce company adopted a network monitoring solution that used machine learning algorithms to analyze historical data and predict traffic spikes. This system was integrated with the company's SDN infrastructure, allowing the monitoring solution to dynamically adjust traffic flows and optimize resource allocation during peak times. The ability to predict traffic surges in advance allowed the company to allocate additional resources to high-demand areas, such as web servers and databases, before issues arose. This proactive approach ensured that the network remained stable and responsive, even during periods of extremely high demand.

In addition to improving network performance, the company also enhanced its monitoring capabilities by integrating real-time application monitoring. This integration provided detailed insights into how application performance was impacted by network conditions, allowing the company to pinpoint issues such as slow-loading pages or transaction delays. By combining network and application monitoring, the company was able to optimize the entire end-to-end user experience, ensuring that customers had a seamless and fast shopping experience, even during the busiest times of the year.

These case studies illustrate how network monitoring has evolved to meet the demands of modern, dynamic environments. Both service providers and enterprises face unique challenges, but the integration of advanced monitoring protocols, machine learning, and cloud-native solutions has enabled them to overcome these challenges and improve performance, security, and customer experience. Whether it is through the use of real-time telemetry data, predictive analytics, or better integration across cloud and on-prem environments, modern network monitoring solutions are helping organizations remain agile, efficient, and responsive in an increasingly complex digital landscape.

Designing a Resilient Network Monitoring Strategy

A resilient network monitoring strategy is crucial for ensuring that an organization's network infrastructure remains operational, secure, and efficient in the face of increasing complexity and evolving challenges. In a world where downtime can result in significant financial losses and security breaches can lead to irreparable damage to an organization's reputation, having a robust monitoring strategy is no longer optional but a necessity. Designing such a strategy requires a careful balance between comprehensive visibility, scalability, reliability, and real-time responsiveness to ensure that the network operates at peak performance and security at all times.

The first step in designing a resilient network monitoring strategy is to establish clear objectives and understand the unique requirements of the network. A well-defined strategy should align with the organization's business goals, ensuring that monitoring efforts contribute directly to the overall success of the organization. Different types of networks, whether corporate networks, data centers, service provider networks, or cloud infrastructures, have distinct characteristics and demands. For example, a large enterprise network may prioritize security and compliance, while a cloud provider's infrastructure may emphasize scalability and performance optimization. Understanding these needs is essential for determining which network metrics to focus on, the monitoring tools to deploy, and the response mechanisms to establish.

One of the cornerstones of a resilient network monitoring strategy is visibility. Without clear and comprehensive visibility into the network, organizations cannot detect issues in a timely manner or respond effectively. To ensure that the monitoring system provides full coverage, it should be capable of tracking a broad range of performance metrics, including bandwidth usage, latency, packet loss, error rates, CPU and memory utilization, and application performance. Monitoring tools should be able to aggregate data from diverse sources such as network devices, firewalls, servers, cloud services, and applications. This visibility should be continuous, allowing administrators to gain real-time insights into network health and performance. A network monitoring strategy must also encompass both physical and virtual components, including SDN controllers, cloud resources, and even edge devices, which are increasingly becoming a part of the modern enterprise network.

Once visibility is established, scalability becomes a critical factor. Networks are continuously growing, whether through the addition of new users, devices, services, or geographical locations. A resilient monitoring strategy must be able to scale as the network expands. This includes having the infrastructure and tools in place to manage large volumes of data generated by an increasingly complex network. Scalable monitoring solutions can accommodate growth without compromising on performance or accuracy. Cloud-based monitoring systems, for example, can automatically scale to handle increased traffic and additional devices, making them a flexible and cost-effective option for modern network environments. These systems can collect data in real-time, provide analytics, and scale as needed without requiring significant hardware upgrades or system overhauls.

Automation plays a significant role in ensuring the resilience of a network monitoring strategy. As networks grow in size and complexity, the amount of data to be analyzed can overwhelm manual processes. Automated monitoring tools can help by performing continuous checks on network performance, alerting administrators to issues before they affect users or services. Automation can also streamline responses to common network issues. For instance, when a specific threshold is reached, the system can automatically trigger predefined actions, such as rerouting traffic, increasing bandwidth, or restarting a malfunctioning device. This proactive approach reduces response time and helps maintain network stability without requiring constant human intervention.

Another essential element of a resilient network monitoring strategy is fault tolerance. A network monitoring system must be designed to continue functioning even when individual components fail or experience issues. This means that monitoring systems should be redundant, with backup systems in place to ensure that data collection and analysis can continue uninterrupted. Redundancy should be built into both the monitoring tools and the underlying infrastructure. For example, monitoring systems can be distributed across multiple servers or locations to ensure that a failure in one part of the system does not bring down the entire monitoring platform. This redundancy is especially important for organizations that rely on 24/7 uptime and cannot afford to have their monitoring systems down for even a short period.

Resilience also requires the ability to respond to incidents effectively. A monitoring strategy should include a clear incident response plan that outlines the steps to be taken when a network issue or security incident is detected. This plan should include defined roles and responsibilities, communication protocols, and escalation procedures to ensure that issues are addressed quickly and efficiently. Moreover, network monitoring should integrate with other operational systems, such as ticketing systems, security information and event management (SIEM) platforms, and configuration management tools, to provide a holistic response to incidents. When a problem is detected, automated alerts should trigger immediate responses, such as logging incidents, notifying the appropriate teams, or initiating remediation workflows. This integration of monitoring with broader operational systems ensures that network resilience is maintained even during periods of high stress or during a security breach.

Security is another critical consideration when designing a resilient network monitoring strategy. Network monitoring tools not only provide insights into network performance but also play an essential role in identifying security threats and vulnerabilities. A resilient strategy must include robust security monitoring capabilities that can detect and respond to a wide range of potential security threats, such as Distributed Denial of Service (DDoS) attacks, unauthorized access attempts, and malware infections. Security monitoring tools should be integrated with the broader network monitoring system to ensure that security incidents are detected and responded to in real time. Additionally, encryption, authentication, and access controls should be in place to protect monitoring data and ensure that sensitive information is kept secure.

Data retention is also an important aspect of network monitoring resilience. The monitoring system should not only capture real-time data but also store it for historical analysis, trend identification, and auditing purposes. This historical data is essential for understanding network performance over time, identifying long-term patterns, and predicting future network needs. A resilient monitoring strategy should include a well-defined data retention policy that ensures that data is kept for the appropriate duration while balancing storage needs and compliance requirements. Additionally, the monitoring system should be able to quickly retrieve and analyze historical data to aid in troubleshooting and root cause analysis during incidents.

In addition to technical resilience, organizational factors must also be considered when designing a network monitoring strategy. The organization must have the right skills, processes, and governance structures in place to ensure that the monitoring strategy is effective. This includes training staff on how to use monitoring tools, interpret alerts, and respond to network issues. It also requires establishing clear policies and procedures for maintaining and updating the monitoring system as the network evolves. Governance is essential for ensuring that monitoring systems align with regulatory requirements, security best practices, and organizational objectives.

Designing a resilient network monitoring strategy is an ongoing process that requires careful planning, investment in the right tools, and a proactive approach to maintenance and improvement. As networks continue to grow in complexity and importance, organizations must ensure that their monitoring strategies evolve alongside these changes, enabling them to maintain high performance, security, and availability at all times. With a robust, resilient monitoring system in place, organizations can navigate the challenges of modern networking environments and maintain operational excellence.

www.ingramcontent.com/pod-product-compliance
Lightning Source LLC
LaVergne TN
LVHW051234050326
832903LV00028B/2395